Praise for *The High Roller Experience*

"As an outstanding and very active board member, David Norton helped create billions of dollars of equity value across several of our companies. *The High Roller Experience* is an engaging treatise from a master of brand building, customer analytics, and all it takes to effectively grow your business."
> —Craig Frances, Managing Director at Summit Partners

"Very few firms can point to a customer-centric transformation that is as comprehensive and successful as what Harrah's/Caesars went through—and very few people were as central to that transformation as David Norton was. This is a must-read for any executive that wants to achieve similar kinds of customer-centric success."
> —Peter S. Fader, Frances and Pei-Yuan Chia Professor of Marketing at the Wharton School of the University of Pennsylvania

"A great loyalty program profitably influences customer behavior by encouraging incremental activity without underwriting existing business. David Norton, my colleague at Caesars for many years, provides the lessons from years of experience in building the organizational capacity to deliver world-class customer loyalty."
> —Gary Loveman, President of Healthagen, Executive Vice President of Aetna, and former executive officer of Caesars Entertainment Corporation

"David Norton unveils the numerous secrets of casino-industry loyalty programs. All companies could benefit from this comprehensive review."
> —Al Ries, bestselling coauthor of *Positioning*

"*The High Roller Experience* provides fascinating detail on the Harrah's marketing story with insight on the analytic and organizational processes that enabled such a transformative change in the casino industry. It is also interesting to see the applicability of the strategy to so many other industries and to see how digital and big data technology have advanced and how sophisticated the approach is at GALE Partners."
> —Felix Rappaport, President of Foxwoods
> Resort and Casino

"This book is a must for those who want to improve the customer experience and marketing effectiveness in their company by using data and digital technology. There are practical examples and lessons learned of how to approach driving transformational change, even in the most complex of organizations. I have known David for many years, originally in his role as a board member of NVA who helped enhance our marketing approach, and I knew some of his story, but I found the details and multiple case study examples to be both compelling and fun to read."
> —Greg Hartmann, CEO of National Veterinary Associates

"In a marketing age focused on 'personalization at scale,' David Norton presents a fascinating look at how he has spearheaded advances in CRM and loyalty management using data, experimentation, and agility long before such terms were mainstream. Beyond the strategic and tactical discussions about data and offers, he provides specificity on how to incorporate these decisions into an overall company strategy and push past organizational resistance."
> —Matthew J. Quint, Director, Center on Global Brand
> Leadership, Columbia Business School

THE
HIGH
ROLLER
EXPERIENCE

HOW CAESARS
AND OTHER
WORLD-CLASS
COMPANIES ARE
USING DATA
TO CREATE AN
UNFORGETTABLE
CUSTOMER EXPERIENCE

DAVID **NORTON**

**Mc
Graw
Hill
Education**

New York   Chicago   San Francisco   Athens   London   Madrid
Mexico City   Milan   New Delhi   Singapore   Sydney Toronto

Thank you to my family (Kristin, Sophie, Owen, and Charlie)
for their love and support as I have traveled the country and the world
chasing my dreams. And to all of you I have worked with over the years;
thank you for making the journey intellectually stimulating and fun,
especially the teams at Harrah's and GALE.

1 2 3 4 5 6 7 8 9   QFR   22 21 20 19 18 17

ISBN   978-1-259-86295-3
MHID   1-259-86295-X

e-ISBN   978-1-259-86296-0
e-MHID   1-259-86296-8

This publication is designed to provide accurate and authoritative information in regard to the subject matter covered. It is sold with the understanding that neither the author nor the publisher is engaged in rendering legal, accounting, securities trading, or other professional services. If legal advice or other expert assistance is required, the services of a competent professional person should be sought.

—From a Declaration of Principles Jointly Adopted
by a Committee of the American Bar Association and
a Committee of Publishers and Associations

Library of Congress Cataloging-in-Publication Data
Names: Norton, David (David William), author.
Title: The high roller experience : how Caesars and other world-class
   companies are using data to create an unforgettable customer experience /
   David Norton.
Description: New York : McGraw-Hill, [2018]
Identifiers: LCCN 2017027994| ISBN 9781259862953 (alk. paper) | ISBN
   125986295X
Subjects: LCSH: Customer relations. | Consumer profiling. | Customer loyalty.
Classification: LCC HF5415.5 .N67 2018 | DDC 658.8/34—dc23 LC record
available at https://lccn.loc.gov/2017027994

McGraw-Hill Education books are available at special quantity discounts to use as premiums and sales promotions or for use in corporate training programs. To contact a representative, please visit the Contact Us page at www.mhprofessional.com.

CONTENTS

PART 3
The Proliferation of Digital and Big Data

PRELUDE

During my time at Harrah's and Caesars, we had numerous great companies spend time with us in Las Vegas to discuss marketing and the customer experience. They were intrigued by the way the casino industry manages its best customers, and they had read about our broader success in marketing as well. These meetings were always intellectually stimulating as we discussed what the visiting companies were doing well that could help us improve some element of our business, and we collectively developed a road map for how they could make progress in CRM, analytics, and loyalty. The most amusing and telling way the CMO from one of these companies summarized his emotions after the session was over was that he was "both impressed and depressed"—impressed upon learning what we were doing from a marketing perspective and driving an enhanced customer experience throughout the casino resort, and depressed by the realization that he had a lot of work to do within his own firm to replicate that success.

These meetings made me realize that the things that we were doing in the casino business at Harrah's were applicable across a range of industries and could be applied at many great companies, especially those whose expertise had been focused on brand management, product development, and operations. I am also constantly amazed at how many people are familiar with and respect the Harrah's marketing story, particularly if they had studied the Harvard Business School case in their MBA program, and are eager to learn the details. The ability to translate that knowledge to their own environment is compelling for people to hear as well. These numerous interactions drew me to the consulting and agency side, as I realized there was a lot of potential to work collaboratively with smart and progressive clients to help them achieve excellence in customer centricity relatively quickly.

To scale and expand the offering, we decided to create GALE, building a team of people with a broad array of expertise including strategic consulting, digital, and technology acumen. We had several objectives in mind when creating GALE, with a realization that there was a seam in the market that would enable us to deliver unique value to clients. Our mantra was and is to deliver strategic thinking on par with the top consulting firms but with an ability to support ongoing operational execution. Another objective was to be a data-driven agency where science was more dominant than art, and we wanted to focus on helping our clients integrate those insights into their operations very quickly in order drive business value and create internal momentum for change. We also wanted to help our clients avoid the trap of making a seven-figure investment in database or digital technology and not using the functionality fully to personalize the customer experience, so we built platforms that allow our clients to be up and running in a sophisticated way at a fraction of the typical cost and much more quickly. Case studies from our work at GALE provide a tremendous complement to the Harrah's story: they demonstrate how data and science can be used to improve marketing and the customer experience in a broad array of industries, and they prove the power of the latest technology advances. *The High Roller Experience* encapsulates the thinking and experience that will enable rapid growth in profitability and customer satisfaction at your organization and shows you how you can implement it in your own company's marketing and customer-focused strategy.

FOREWORD

In my former role as Managing Director at a global IT services company, I had the opportunity to work with Harrah's/Caesars Entertainment, one of the world's most illustrious gaming companies. The mission was to create a set of systems that would elevate Harrah's/Caesars into a customer experience leadership position in the highly competitive Las Vegas casino space. Championed by the CMO, David Norton, this ambitious task would transform customer centricity in the casino industry.

Today, the fact that CMOs have a strong influence over technology spend is a given, but back then it was unheard of. Pioneering today's CMO model a decade ahead of his time, David was adamant about using data to shape world-class customer experiences, and he was laser-focused on running analytics in the background, while digging deep into the financials to shape better experiences. With his progressive approach, it's no surprise that David received numerous accolades such as CMO of the Year based on the exceptional results he delivers.

Many years later, our paths crossed again over dinner in midtown Manhattan. David was now a Managing Director at MDC Partners, a top marketing and advertising holding company. He wanted to discuss how many companies still struggled to create relevant data-driven customer experiences. This was a common problem across industries, even though today's environment is perfect for the core principles that David developed during his time at Harrah's/Caesars Entertainment. We talked about how expectations for today's consumers were much higher, how consumers had grown much more accepting of brands using data to create great experiences, and how the explosion of mobile and cheap cloud computing could enable personalization like never before.

One spirited conversation over dinner quickly evolved into a set of ongoing idea exchanges over the next few months. The time was right to apply David's extensive experience in the data-rich casino space to new industries, taking advantage of today's technology advancements and the emerging world of data science.

In this book, David not only does a masterful job of outlining the strategic thinking required to create world-class experiences; he also provides tactical recommendations on how to operationalize these insights.

Working together at GALE, David and I have built an agency that is helping today's forward-looking brands create great customer experiences. In creating GALE, we wanted to develop a next-generation agency. In doing so, we knew we would need to apply the rigor and discipline of a management consultancy, while bringing the creativity and empathy of a world-class creative agency. We also knew we needed to be an agency that could bring the right amount of strategy and that could transition that strategy into flawless execution.

With GALE we have successfully, from day one, brought together business strategy, creativity, data, and technology, and are helping brands answer critical business questions like "Who are my best customers and how do I find more of them?" and "How should I invest my marketing spend across customer segments and channels based on competitive dynamics?"

Relevant for marketers across industries, this book goes beyond the casino space to illustrate how you can build great customer experiences and drive ROI in any organization.

Brad Simms

PART 1

A Broader View of Loyalty

L oyalty is about more than a rewards program where customers are fixated on point accumulation and the company is
primarily concerned about the cost of contingent liability. Loyalty
is about understanding your customers in detail and interacting
with them in a highly personalized way at every point of contact
with your brand.

A Road Map to Success

Many companies state they have a customer focus as one of their
key mantras to drive market share and profitability. In reality,
this typically only means having a strong customer service culture and the right products, but it does not entail the orientation
and tools to implement a relevant and customer-centric approach
in all marketing activities and service touchpoints. A shocking
number of highly successful companies are still in the very early
stages of developing CRM (customer relationship management)
and loyalty tools, unable to make progress that would improve
customer satisfaction and marketing efficiency, and, of course,
ultimately improve financial results.

In this book, *The High Roller Experience*, we will explore the
reasons that have limited progress on this front and provide you
with a road map and lessons learned that will enable your success. Having met with a number of great companies over the
years, either as part of a daylong info share or through more
extensive consulting engagements, we can see clearly that there

is a remarkably common set of challenges that limit progress, and it is equally clear that there are huge opportunities to drive transformative change. There are organizational and talent barriers that make it difficult to succeed, and historically there have not been great external solutions that can both tell clients what to do as well as how to execute it operationally with hardware and software—not to mention the talent that is required to do so.

CMOs are pressured to deliver short-term results, so when push comes to shove, their bias will be to focus on what they need to do in the immediate here and now, as opposed to spending time on longer-term capability building initiatives. They also often don't have experience leading the building of technical capabilities, and they may not have the funding from their organization to resource properly against more expensive projects. CEOs are more focused on financial results, employee issues, and product decisions, and many of them don't support CRM efforts as vigorously as they could to push organizational transformation focused on customer centricity.

One of the bigger obstacles to success is a company's technical infrastructure; primarily this means not having all the necessary data in one accessible spot to fully understand the customer. Marketers in many instances don't have the ability to use all the data they would like to use because it is in various databases that can't be accessed in marketing queries and analysis. This is especially true for companies that have made a meaningful number of acquisitions over the years or have a wide variety of product lines where customer data is siloed, as these companies have likely not been able to create an integrated view of the customer. Investing in this database step is essential, though many companies are paralyzed by the complexity of big data.

The terms *CRM* and *customer centricity* have been used liberally and loosely by tech and consulting companies as well as those that write about them, all of which leads to confusion among decision makers. A customer-centric organization executes against many different marketing and operational components including the following:

- Deploys a sophisticated, closed-loop, highly segmented direct marketing process

- Conducts robust analysis

- Offers a compelling loyalty structure with differentiated service and benefits and a strong customer value proposition

- Has a deep understanding of the intersection of product performance and customer segmentation

- Delivers personalized experiences in multiple touchpoints seamlessly

Many companies do one or two of these components quite well; for example, airlines and hotels have very successful loyalty programs, but typically they don't engage in sophisticated CRM. Many companies have very basic segmentation schemes for direct marketing, but they don't have an ability to provide continuity across channels and provide a seamless customer experience.

Companies also struggle with the idea that customer centricity is a journey that requires iterative progress to build momentum internally and to evolve an organization's culture. While there may be a grandiose vision of what the goal is, it is impossible to get there immediately in one step. As cliché as it is, the lowest-hanging fruit should be identified and harvested to prove the impact as quickly as possible. Constantly evolving and rolling out more sophisticated functionality can be done over time as the organization sees the quantifiable benefit of data-driven and customer-centric marketing.

I have been fortunate to work with companies where customer loyalty is core to the firm's DNA, starting with financial services at MBNA and American Express; and then for 12 years at Harrah's/Caesars Entertainment where I was the architect of Total Rewards, which is widely viewed as one of the best loyalty programs in the world.

More recently, I have been able to work with great clients from a wide range of industries that are looking to enhance their loyalty capabilities and relationships with customers. Finally, as a frequent business traveler, I get to experience airline, hotel, and car rental loyalty programs from a consumer's perspective. These experiences have all built upon one another to inform the expertise that is shared in this book.

In Part 1, I offer a deep look into the development and evolution of Total Rewards, one of the most recognized loyalty schemes in the world, as never before told, and I give examples of creating innovative loyalty mechanisms across a range of diverse industries. You will see why loyalty goes well beyond a point-based program and entails engaging with customers in a contextually relevant way across a variety of touchpoints.

Customer Centricity and All Its Components

M ost companies are organized by product line, business unit, or geography and find it very challenging to take a customer-centric approach to running their business. The customer is a by-product of the organization's design as opposed to being the core around which the company operates. Customer centricity means that the customer is the company's and not an individual business unit's. It is an ability to interact with the customer cohesively and consistently regardless of which business unit the customer is dealing with. Customers increasingly have this expectation of the brands they buy from, and they are unaware of and don't care about organizational silos.

Customer centricity does not entail simply implementing a CRM tool and software. Rather it is an integrated approach to managing one's business, including having a thorough understanding of the customer and the ability to take refined actions in a multitude of service and marketing touchpoints—increasingly in real time via mobile leveraging digital technologies. It requires constant refinement and evolution over an extended period of time based on sophisticated analytics while simultaneously driving meaningful incremental results for the business.

It is surprising to me how many great companies don't have a customer segmentation scheme in place. This is a critical way to understand the motivations, needs, and profitability of your customer base in a logical way but more importantly should be a way to interact with customers in the most relevant way. Many companies do have some form of strategic segmentation that helps prioritize investment and helps employees understand the relative value and personas of customers. However, it is even more critical to have a tactical segmentation methodology that can be used in direct marketing or real time on the web or in mobile marketing to be contextually relevant and to more effectively utilize distressed inventory. Too many companies use a one-size-fits-all approach in direct marketing and email as it relates to messaging, frequency, and channel of contact and incentive type or amount. Personalizing the marketing communication approach will dramatically improve the efficiency of marketing spend both by eliminating activities that will not be fruitful and by improving response through more appropriate offers. And customers will be much happier when their inboxes aren't flooded with extraneous messages and when the communication they do get is more relevant.

There Is a Time and Place for Strategic Segmentation

While I have a strong preference for using detailed customer-level data to create an actionable tactical segmentation, there is a time and place for strategic segmentation that helps inform higher-level decision making. Many companies use one of the well-known psychographic profiles such as Personix obtained from third parties which helps people think about key customer profiles with the very descriptive and amusing names. However, it is often not very actionable as it relates to targeted marketing, as it is costly to score your entire database, and more crucially, it is hard to change someone's profile. We saw an example of this recently: a large consulting firm had created five segments that were labeled with five female names for one of our retail clients. Unfortunately the names did not provide intuitive insight into the characteristics of each segment that would help marketing or operations know what to do differently for each persona without diving into more detail.

In 2010, we did a very powerful strategic segmentation project at Harrah's. It was part of our effort to drive new business to fill the significant revenue gap we had from the decline in play from our VIP customers after the economic crisis of September 2008. We conducted a deep research effort to understand the total travel and entertainment (T&E) spend from a variety of customers, including VIPs and non-VIPs, loyal and nonloyal customers, and a significant group of non–Total Rewards members. This exhaustive survey helped us think about the opportunity much more broadly than just gaming revenue. As we obtained insight into consumers spend on dining, entertainment, and other leisure activities, we realized what a small percentage of T&E spend we were capturing with our gaming-focused marketing tactics considering the vast array of excellent assets we had at our disposal. We gained insight into segments where we were overpenetrated compared with the competition, such as "comp connoisseurs," given the power of our loyalty program. And we identified those segments where we had less than our fair share given our competitors' investment in nongaming assets relative to ours. The research effort told us of the potential value for each segment from both a gaming and nongaming perspective to help us quantify the potential and to help rally the organization around the need to evolve around our core gaming customer (see Figure 1.1).

From this work we created segments for both our frequency and destination markets and realized at what rate the same customers have one personality when they visit a casino regularly in their hometown as opposed to making an annual visit to Las Vegas. In the local market the motivation is often a gaming-centric night out, while the Vegas trip is much more diverse in its objectives to enjoy world-class entertainment, shopping, and dining.

FIGURE 1.1	Strategic segments and their value

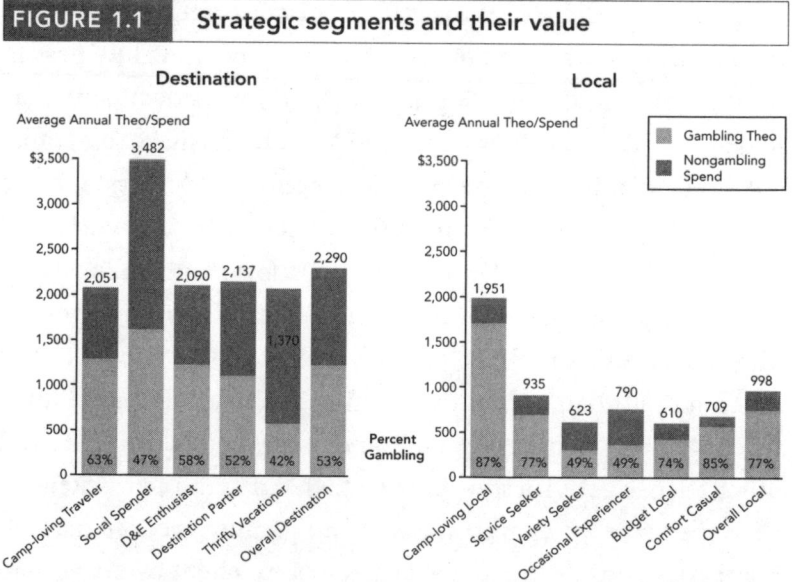

The implications of this work were quite broad for the key markets we specifically focused on, including where we spent our traditional media dollars and as an input on where and how to invest capital. While it was not feasible to score the whole database with these segments to execute against them in our direct marketing, the value of the project far exceeded my expectations.

Taking a Differentiated Approach to Market Segmentation

A more sophisticated segmentation approach certainly leads to more clerical work internally and with a company's production execution vendors. So as basic as it seems, you must do something different for each segment if you are going to put forth the effort to segment, whether that is varying content in the form of images and copy or the promotional incentive type and amount. In addition, it is very important to automate the segmentation queries and negate manual ad hoc queries so that marketing resources can spend the majority of their time thinking about what to do based on recent results and market dynamics as opposed to spending all their time on the tactical aspects of executing. It is also important to maintain some stability over time in the segmentation both to create a longitudinal history to compare results and to minimize rework for vendors as they execute.

Customers will move in and out of segments as their behavior changes, but the segments should stay constant for at least 12 to 18 months, assuming there are no dramatic changes in the business or competitive landscape. How often customers should be rescored is a function of the frequency with which customers engage with the brand; we have seen clients rescore their customers anywhere from twice a year to several times a week. This also mitigates any rework for vendors or internal partners and reduces the risk of errors they may make that can have a significant negative impact on the business.

We experienced a major mistake by a direct mail vendor during my Harrah's days when the vendor inverted the offer matrix, meaning that the lower-value customers got the best customers' offers and our high-daily-spend customers got very modest offers meant for the masses. To exacerbate the problem, there were many more customers in the low-value category than in the VIP level; as a result, our financial exposure was several million dollars, because the state where the casino was located made us honor the erroneous coupon values. This error led us to dramatically reduce the number of suppliers we used and increase the amount of insurance we had in place to protect ourselves from mistakes going forward.

The Importance of Test and Control Cells

An ability to easily have test and control cells as part of the execution process is very important too. Marketers should be able to quickly select what percentage of the audience will get the standard offer/creative opposed to the challenger ones and what percentage will be controlled (excluded) from that promotion as well. Being able to rapidly measure test and control results in a timely fashion through standard reports is critical in order to respond and take the appropriate action in short order. Too often companies don't have an automated process in place to measure test and control efforts, and as a result, it takes months to evaluate what happened, making it irrelevant by the time the analysis is done since the competitive landscape has changed.

There are varying philosophies about control groups. Some companies hold a portion of their customer base from all marketing activity, and others do it at a promotion/campaign level. I believe holding out customers from a specific marketing program is much more informative in determining which marketing activities drive the most incremental profitability, changing the customer's behavior to spend more with you than with a competitor. Many companies have universal control groups, which do not enable an understanding of the relative performance of all marketing programs. Understanding incremental profitability and the relative performance of marketing campaigns are more important than estimating the impact of all marketing activity because it allows the company to make surgical changes to optimize marketing spend.

From 1999 to 2008, we conducted a lot of direct marketing tests at Harrah's that improved the effectiveness of our marketing dramatically, but the property marketers were very hesitant to have control groups for fear that they would be threatening their revenue. We were by no means suggesting going dark on our customers. The reality was that instead of getting an average of eight incentives in a month, they would be getting seven. Some customers would be getting offers 1 through 7 and not 8, and others 1 through 6 and 8 but not 7, and so on. Ultimately we were trying to learn a variety of things:

- How many of the eight programs were driving incremental profitability?

- How does the performance of each of the programs compare?

- What is the point of diminishing returns at a customer-segment level; that is, where was promotional activity no longer driving incremental profitability?

- Which types of programs were most relevant to specific customers?

- Which customers were most sensitive to promotional activity?

However, at the beginning of 2009 with the economic crisis impacting customer demand and our profitability, we mandated that control groups be done on all programs so that we could identify ineffective marketing spend and either drop it to the bottom line or reallocate it to more profitable activities. At the same time, we centralized all marketing analysis to ensure that the best decisions were being made, realizing that customers were not as responsive to our marketing programs as they had been in the past. Amazingly, of the dozens of innovations I asked the organization to embrace, centralizing marketing analysis so we could understand this critical information was the easiest one by far. The division presidents simply requested that I resource it appropriately to enable rapid and thorough analysis to help them make marketing decisions. We created a report, shown in Figure 1.2, that evaluated every program a property did in a month; this illustrated which ones were successful in driving incremental

FIGURE 1-2	Program evaluation 2 x 2

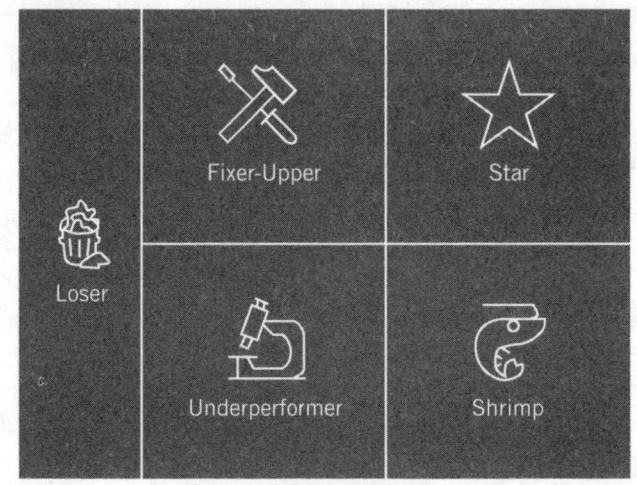

Incremental Profit, Percent
EBITDA Margin

profitability and which ones did not and in essence layered cost to revenue we would have received anyway.

We were able to assess this within a week of the offers expiring, which allowed us to make modifications to the approach very quickly. If the property marketers did not drop or significantly alter their losers, shrimps, and fixer-uppers, we communicated up the chain to get the right outcome. In 2010, we further refined our ability to understand program incrementality at a customer-segment level within a program that enabled us to even more accurately optimize our spend.

Keys to an Effective Segmentation Scheme

Ideally a company has all the needed data in a warehouse and has sophisticated CRM tools to drive the segmentation, but that is often not the case. In the theme of iterative progress, it is perfectly acceptable to start with a basic segmentation approach that will drive meaningful differentiation in messaging/creative/offers to different groups of customers.

Our first wave of segmentation at Harrah's was based on four stages of the customer life cycle (new, nonloyal, loyal, and defector), but our offer approach and messaging were dramatically different by segment. At a retail client I engaged with, the initial segmentation was to distinguish the client's core lower-end and mid-tier customers from its emerging higher-end ones in direct marketing, on the web, and in store to match the right product and pricing so as not to alienate the core audience with the unapproachable products nor the customers in the new aspirational segment with a product that was too low quality for their taste. This type of segmentation can be done by creating flags at a guest level that can be easily accessed at time of query using a standard tool such as Cognos or MicroStrategy.

There is a lot of talk about one-to-one marketing, but the key to an effective segmentation scheme is having an ability to execute feasibly within the organizational construct, as there is an executional burden of having more versions of emails or direct mail pieces. It is critical to prioritize the lowest-hanging fruit segments and then determine how the copy, images, and incentive will vary by segment to drive different behavior (see Figure 1.3). At GALE, we believe microclustering is the sweet spot of a sophisticated segment scheme that can be executed. You should not be embarrassed by having a basic segmentation approach to start with if it will make a difference in how you will communicate and incent customers, as ultimately there should be a lift in the key metrics that are used to evaluate marketing programs such as open and click-through rates and, of course, revenue per contact.

At Harrah's we started with the basic life cycle approach: new business, nonloyal, loyal, and defector, as a way to improve our marketing effectiveness. Previously the vast majority of our marketing expense was being directed to our most loyal customers, as is the case with most organizations. Of course, targeting these

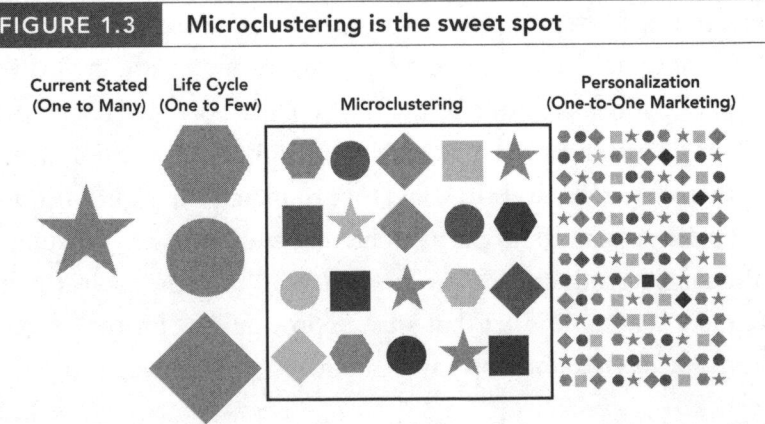

FIGURE 1.3   **Microclustering is the sweet spot**

customers led to higher response rates, but we also felt that there were other reasons besides incentives that they were visiting us, such as our being their most proximate casino option, the superior service they received, their rapport with specific employees, and, once we added tiers, the service benefits they received at the higher-tier levels. Our goal was to reduce the offer and discount spend as a percentage of revenue slightly in the loyal segment and reallocate the promotional dollars to the other segments that we thought had more upside potential. Dave Kowal on my team would often say that response rates and incrementality were inversely related, which was an extreme point of view but also had a lot of merit.

The objectives for the other segments were quite purposeful as well. For the new-business segment, two of our objectives were to welcome new members and educate them about the Total Rewards program and its distribution of properties and brands. A third objective was to aggressively incent a second trip to one of our properties, especially for those customers that we predicted had significant upside, since we had found that generating a repeat visit led to regular visits going forward.

Another critical segment for us to focus on was the nonloyal group of customers, as that is where the most potential was to steal share. By providing increased value for more frequent visits, we saw a significant increase in revenue from this group that we predicted were only giving us a fraction of their casino trips.

The final segment from the original scheme was defectors. The big change we made was to identify more quickly those customers who had broken their typical visitation pattern as opposed to the standard inactive program practice of waiting 6 or 12 months to reach out to them, at which time they would have been long gone. For example, with our new approach if customers came every week historically but we had not seen them for several weeks, they were flagged as defectors. For those customers that came monthly, they were identified as defectors if we had not seen them for two months. This enabled us to connect with the customers who had been frequent visitors and encourage them to come back before they had become loyal to one of our competitors. It also ensured that we did not get unnecessarily aggressive with discounts and send the wrong message to customers who came periodically.

Our goal was to create an automated closed-loop marketing process that provided a consistent approach for all our properties but varied appropriately based on unique market dynamics (see Figure 1.4). Enabling the properties to get a high degree of segmentation and robust reporting at a click of a button allowed them to spend more time thinking about what to do rather than spending all their time creating queries and reports to execute basic marketing.

Evolving Segmentation Strategy to Maximize Marketing Effectiveness

Our segmentation evolved in many ways after the initial life cycle approach to increase the relevance and effectiveness of our marketing. We calculated implied preferences with our rich information about what customers did on their visits to our properties, including games played, offers redeemed, and nongaming activities, and we stored the preferences at a customer level for easy use in campaigns. We noted whether the customers preferred slot or table games, if they participated in gaming tournaments, if they most often came midweek or on the weekend, how often they redeemed our offers when they came, what type of entertainment they preferred, which channel of communication they preferred, and a host of other factors. We used these implied preferences as inclusion and exclusion rules in campaigns. By excluding customers from programs that they had no chance to respond to

FIGURE 1.4	Closed-loop CRM approach

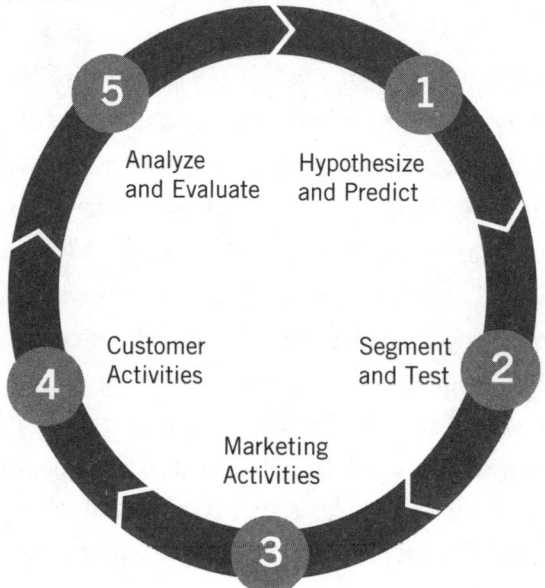

Segmenting for Action

- Consistent and repeatable
- Actionable—different messaging, incentive amount/type, creative
- Stage of life cycle, daily, annual, and lifetime value
- Predicted share of wallet
- Multiproduct purchaser
- Customer-centric contact controls
- Many small segments more realistic than one to one
- Implied preferences versus stated
- Transactional data was much more fruitful than external data sources
- Don't swing the pendulum on incentives
- Analyze business by many customer segments in automated fashion
- Understand program performance

based on their past behavior, we dramatically improved response rates and cost savings. And we made our customers happier.

Leveraging Customer Performance Information

The last several pages have detailed how segmentation is used in the tactical execution of CRM, but understanding customer performance should also be used to drive the strategy of the business. When I started at Harrah's, the company's focus was on what we called "Avid Experienced Slot Customers," those who lost on average more than $200 per trip, which contributed the vast majority of our revenue. As we aimed to grow our revenue, we considered the notion of evolving around the core customer base. So when we changed Total Rewards dramatically in 2003, one of our key objectives was to bring more value both to table games customers of all levels and to high-frequency, lower-daily-value slot customers.

The next significant customer segment that we wanted to attract was domestic Asian customers when we developed a robust multicultural marketing function; we also focused on attracting cash-paying entertainment seekers when we began tracking non-gaming spend in Total Rewards. In addition to building marketing and operational capabilities to attract these customer segments efficiently and service them well, our analytic capabilities enabled us to evaluate our performance against these segments by property to create benchmarks and goals across the enterprise.

We further enhanced our ability to attract high-spending, cash-paying customers with something we called Total Experiences. After the economic crisis in the fall of 2008, we saw a significant decline in revenue from our gaming customers, and we were looking to backfill some of that revenue. We were still running at a very high occupancy rate in Las Vegas and our other destination markets, but more rooms were being booked to lower-value guests, including a higher percentage through third-party sources like Expedia, Travelocity, and others, where the profit margin was modest for us given the fees we had to pay them and the bargain-seeking customer they attracted.

We knew that Las Vegas was very popular for a variety of small-group occasions such as bachelor and bachelorette parties, guys' golf weekends, girls' weekends, and, of course, weddings. However, we discovered that it was very difficult to book hotel rooms and the other activities for small groups through our service touchpoints, as our web booking engine was for individual reservations and the group meeting function was for much larger business meetings. We also knew that there was a lot of pressure for the group organizer, who likely was very time constrained based on professional and other responsibilities at home, and not fully informed about all the amenities available in our portfolio or Las Vegas more broadly, to make all the best decisions for the group. And reminiscent of the scene from the *Hangover* when the boys arrive at Caesars Palace and Doug has to use his card to check in when the others get alligator arms, the organizer does not want to be on the hook for the bill for the entire group.

There were several other critical factors that led us to pursue Total Experiences. The first is that we knew we had fantastic assets in our portfolio that in some instances were reserved only for high rollers. These luxury amenities could command a premium price based on their quality; they included two amazing golf courses, one of which houses Butch Harmon's Teaching Academy; world-class celebrity chef run restaurants; an incredible spa at Caesars Palace; luxury shopping; and some of the best entertainers in the world, such as Céline Dion and Elton John. The second insight was that there was a tremendous amount of mystique about the "high roller experience" that normal casino visitors were interested in experiencing. The general visitors were also curious about the more obvious service benefits that our Seven Stars and Diamond customers received based on what they observed throughout the resort. Finally, we knew we had an ability to execute a high-end service experience like few other resorts in the world. It was something we did every day with our VIP gamers that could be modified for groups of people that collectively were going to spend well more than several thousand dollars on their trip even if most of it was on nongaming activities.

Our next step was to seize the opportunity by occasion primarily for Las Vegas, though we also felt there was an opportunity in Atlantic City, New Orleans, and Lake Tahoe. We were able to quantify the revenue for weddings, bachelor and bachelorette parties, and guys' and girls' getaway weekends and estimate the share we were capturing. With weddings, as an example, the revenue we received from the ceremony across our various Las Vegas properties was ample, but we were capturing very little revenue from all the other wedding activities such as the rehearsal dinner, the bride and bridesmaids getting their hair and nails done, or the guys golfing. We felt there was a significant incremental revenue opportunity by developing sales, marketing, and operational processes to increase consumer awareness and create a seamless booking and service experience.

We then needed to talk to the operators about how to make this a reality. Like the response to many of our ideas, the initial reaction was to doubt the opportunity and raise all the reasons that it could not or should not happen. We heard about our high occupancy rates, even though the last 20 percent of the rooms were marginally profitable based on the level of customer that was getting access. People questioned whether the revenue from these small groups of high-end cash-paying customers would be incremental and whether we could service them properly. For example, given our situation, we didn't have time to build new, elegant technical solutions to enhance the booking process, so there was concern about how manual some of the processes would be, which was a fair concern. Fortunately, several people at Caesars Palace in particular were very willing partners and were instrumental in creating the customer experience during the booking process and once the customers arrived.

After we got the go-ahead, we then focused on how to find customers and communicate the value proposition. We developed the brand positioning, Total Experiences, building on the equity of Total Rewards. I put a smart and charismatic leader in charge of this effort, Veronica Glazer, whose primary task was to focus on bringing this idea to life with the operators. We built the marketing collateral and website to market the offering to customers and employees.

We also felt it was important to build a sales team to find new customers, just as we did on the gaming side, to provide a critical channel. We hired people with nongaming sales experience, particularly those who had worked with high-net-worth individuals, in key feeder markets like New York City, Chicago, Los Angeles, and San Francisco. We had them share space with those who "hunted" for gamers in those markets as well as those who focused on group meetings to create more of a team environment, to share best practices, and to drive synergy from a sales leadership perspective. In New York and Chicago, we invested in attractive office space where we could host customer events, the purpose being to immerse customers in our brand experience.

We were able to make Total Experiences a profitable endeavor within a year and a fairly significant revenue stream for us. This capability still persists and is vibrant for Caesars and has been replicated by the other luxury properties in Las Vegas.

There is no doubt that we were very fortunate to have so much rich data about our customers that we could leverage in our marketing activities, and I realize that most companies are not in the same position, as they have information about their customers in multiple disparate systems that aren't accessible to marketers. I have seen this situation multiple times with clients who often are considering a long and costly project to build a customer database. To get value more quickly, we have gone through a process of first identifying the key data that marketing would like to know about customers to improve personalization efforts and then prioritizing the data by expected value and level of effort to make the data accessible to marketing. Starting with four or five of the desired elements out of a list of twenty is a reasonable place to initiate the personalization journey and build the case and fund investment in the required technology. Using the 3 x 3 matrix (as 2 x 2's are so routine) in Table 1.1 can help prioritize which data to access.

TABLE 1.1	Initiative Prioritization		

		Value		
		Low	Medium	High
	Low			Start Here
Level of Effort	Medium			
	High			

We have seen several clients invest in building "data lakes" recently as a means to getting the most important customer data available to marketing, finance, and operations. On a couple of occasions, we have been first to fully leverage the data in our work with clients, helping them prove the value of their investment as well as helping them learn what data is most valuable. As we engage with their customers in various touchpoints, we feed data back into the data lake, enabling the clients to continue to build a richer profile of their customers and determine what data really matters when creating more relevant content for customers.

In this chapter, we have talked about putting the customer at the core of all business decisions regardless of organizational silos. It is critical to create a segmentation scheme that allows marketers and operators to deliver personalized experiences in a way that can be consistently executed. It is critical to organize and resource around key customer cohorts and create performance measurement tools that create ownership and drive the right actions. Finally, it is imperative to evolve the segmentation approach based on learnings and changes in competitive dynamics. These are the pillars of an effective customer-centric strategy.

Doubling Down

- **Start with a tactical segmentation.** A tactical segmentation primarily built on transactional data is the most effective way to drive improved marketing results. This allows you to meaningfully vary the approach for each customer group.

- **Don't let strategic segmentation drive communication strategy.** There is an important place for strategic segmentation, which generally buckets customers based on research data. However, in most instances, it should not be relied upon to drive customer-specific communication.

- **Test! Test! Test!** Constantly testing and learning and holding out control groups is the best way to optimize marketing spend. This allows companies to find the most appropriate message and to spend resources at a much more refined customer-segment level.

- **Don't stop innovating.** It is critical that you constantly evolve and innovate your segmentation approach to stay ahead of the competition.

Loyalty Programs

There is no doubt that loyalty programs have become ubiquitous and represent a significant amount of expense for companies in many industries. From a consumer point of view, customers are in an average of 18 programs in their quest to earn value from their everyday spend, though the reality is they can only actively engage in about a third of them based on their own time constraints. These dynamics lead to billions of dollars of underutilized point expense and a complexity to programs that is not valued by its participants.

It is apparent that loyalty programs are required to compete in the airline, hotel, and casino industries, as customers expect to be rewarded with free flights and rooms, upgrades, and complimentary meals among other things. In other industries, such as retail, loyalty programs aren't as common, and promotional discounting is the primary lever to drive revenue and steal share. Regardless of the circumstance, there are several principles that should be followed to maximize the value of a loyalty mechanism both for the customer in the form of differentiated service, personalized offers, and rewards and for the company to garner incremental share from its customers.

The Importance of Creating a Differentiated Service Experience

Creating a differentiated service experience is paramount to having an efficient loyalty scheme, as the perceived value can be much higher than the cost to deliver the service if properly conceived, and the cost will not be linear to the revenue generated by the customer. Airline programs do this very well with their tier benefits such as early boarding, the chance to be upgraded, and shorter security lines that enhance the travel experience. A mix of service items and access to unique "priceless" experiences should be developed as part of a three- to four-tier program depending on the size and distribution of the database. Starting with a smaller number of impactful benefits that can be operationally executed is imperative, and if need be benefits can be added over time and promoted to refresh the program.

Obviously, the objective of tiers is to create transparent goals generally on an annual basis for customers to hit to garner increased share from competitors. Where customers stand should be readily available to them in a variety of touchpoints including the web and a mobile site or app, and customers should be reminded of what they need to do to attain or retain a status, especially as the earning time frame approaches its end. Customers will make slightly irrational decisions to achieve a tier status as the qualification end date nears. How many times have you heard that friends or colleagues have taken a trip in December just to qualify or retain a tier? If you are creating a loyalty program, keep in mind that it is important to downgrade customers who don't maintain their status during the expiry window, as our analysis shows gifted customers continue to spend at a low level. Of course, the rare exception can be made when you know the customers have extenuating circumstances that prevented them from coming/spending as often as they typically had.

The element of a loyalty scheme that requires the most finesse is the points-earning and redemption process, as there is a significant cost associated with it whether it is the hard or opportunity cost of the redemption or the accounting expense of contingent liability. While there is a need to have an earning process that is easily understood to members, points earning should be tied to profitability and, ideally, to incremental behavior even though it adds a level of complexity. As an example, the airlines tying earning miles to the cost of a ticket is a smart move that counterbalances how many miles they give to customers in hub markets where there is a limited alternative choice of airlines. Southwest Airlines earning and redemption are perfectly aligned with the cost of the particular flight and type of fare you are buying or redeeming.

At Harrah's, we tied points earning to profitability even though it inhibits transparency to the customer slightly, a subject of much heated debate when we changed Total Rewards dramatically in 2003. Many people at the company wanted points to be tied to the coin-in a customer played through the slot machine similar to how all our competitors did it, since it is easy for the customer to understand. However, because the hold percent (the amount the casino wins) varies dramatically based on the type of slot machine, the profitability garnered on a customer playing a higher-hold game can be nearly twice as much as it is for a customer playing a lower-hold game for the same amount of money flowing through the game. That variability was significantly more than we could live with when rewarding customers. We lessened the confusion by giving customers multiple ways to find out how many points they had, including right at the game, so they could get a sense for how quickly they were earning points. We were fortunate that we stuck to our guns on this, as we could make changes without the customer knowing explicitly what we had done, which would not have been the case if we had to alter the coin-in needed to get a point, which would have been very obvious.

Deciding to Launch a Points Program

For those companies that don't already have a points-earning process in place but want to engender more loyalty and capture more data to engage in personalized marketing, it is a very difficult choice to launch a points program since it is hard to justify discounting existing revenue in the hope that enough incremental revenue will be generated to offset that expense. This was a similar dynamic to the one I faced when we wanted to start rewarding nongaming (hotel, food, shopping, entertainment, etc.) spend in Total Rewards in 2008. We received $2 billion in this revenue without any kind of a loyalty incentive, and there was going to be a significant cost for rewarding that behavior even though we knew we were receiving a disproportionately low percentage of the customers' spend in this category, especially in Las Vegas and Atlantic City. It was the hardest initiative I tried to get implemented in my tenure, as there was so much resistance and skepticism across the organization, and as a result we launched in a minimalist way that we sustained for several years leading to modest impact.

Since I have been consulting to clients in this situation, my recommendation has been to create a points construct that is focused on rewarding incremental behaviors in a surgical, CRM-enabled way, and not to offer points for existing spend if at all possible, especially if the company is implementing a loyalty program from scratch. While less lucrative to customers, the benefit for the company is that the increased expense will be generated on spend that is much more likely to be incremental. An example of how this could be done in retail is to identify customers who have only bought with you in one category and offer them a combination of points and an attractive offer for purchases in other categories. Customers can also be rewarded points for engaging in social media or referring friends to the brand. To help create more ways for customers to earn a meaningful balance, one can implement the turnkey online mall solutions through companies such as Clarus, Cartera, and Rewards Now, where the points are funded by the merchants when sales are driven their way by your customers.

In fact, with several retailers we work with at GALE, we have recommended not having a points program at all but rather focus on experiences and benefits that are more meaningful to customers—and ultimately less costly to the business. We have worked with brands to develop compelling loyalty experiences focused on showing relevant content across multiple channels, providing early access to new products and distressed merchandise, being able to attend VIP experiences, and other opportunities that our research proved to be much more valuable than points. We still suggest providing a tangible goal to achieve, like earning badges or certificates for activities, such as visiting the store or the website, engaging in the brand's social platforms, and, of course, making purchases. This type of approach appeals to a wide range of customers because it has a gamification component and is attainable and the benefits are attractive to both those who want to have the latest fashion first and those who are more cost constrained and want their budget to stretch as far as possible. In cases where evidence shows that customers value experiences much more than points, this design is a true win-win.

Objections to Points Programs

What is ironic about the objection many retailers have to a points system—especially for those customers who aren't using the store's proprietary card—is how much promotional discounting they do, not to mention how many media dollars they spend in nonmeasurable channels, including circulars or high-end magazine ads, to communicate their brand message. I have found that most retailers don't have an effective process in place to measure promotional discounting, and in some instances it isn't truly treated as a marketing expense. One of my recommendations to retail clients is to take a small portion of the discounting dollars and reallocate that money into a surgical CRM effort such as encouraging the customer to spend in another category than they typically do with the brand. I watched with interest what JCPenney did several years ago to try to change the promotional paradigm in retail, which is engrained in consumers' minds. The early results were certainly a disaster. I think it is likely the company went too far too fast, and an evolution of discounting to CRM could have been more successful than the revolutionary approach Penney's took that impacted the business so dramatically and sent it in a downward spiral.

In addition to creating transparent incentives in tiers and points to drive loyalty, the primary value of having a loyalty program should be to use the detailed customer-level data in a meaningful way. As mentioned before, this is where many companies don't get the value they should, as they are not harnessing the data for informing both short-term, more targeted marketing activities and longer-term strategic decisions. Despite having very powerful programs in the airline and hotel industries, none of those industries execute personalized direct marketing activities, or at best they seem to be emerging with those capabilities.

The Push and Pull of CRM and Loyalty Programs

Grocery stores are also historically an example of a flawed loyalty program construct, as they are discounting the price at the point of sale when the customer has already made a decision. Why wouldn't you provide your phone number or present your keyfob at checkout to get the reduced price? How many customers make their decision on where to get their groceries based on this discount as opposed to going to the store that is closest to them or on their way home from work? To top it off, the stores provide you offers on paper for your next trip. How often do those get thrown out as you leave the store or at the very latest when you unload your groceries? The grocery store model needs to be redefined in general, though there have been tremendous success stories with Tesco and Sainsbury in the United Kingdom, and Kroger has invested significantly with Dunnhumby and has had above-average results.

We talk to our clients constantly about what we call the push and pull of CRM and loyalty programs, meaning that loyalty schemes and CRM should work together synergistically (see Figure 2.1). Tiers in loyalty programs provide the clear goals that encourage loyalty, and CRM activities give incentive in between the tier hurdles. As mentioned earlier, very few companies are doing both well, which is why we develop the strategy and capabilities for our clients to excel in both so they can distinguish themselves as leaders in their industries.

There is no doubt that there are great loyalty programs that consumers absolutely love. These include the various hotel and airline programs as well as American Express's Membership

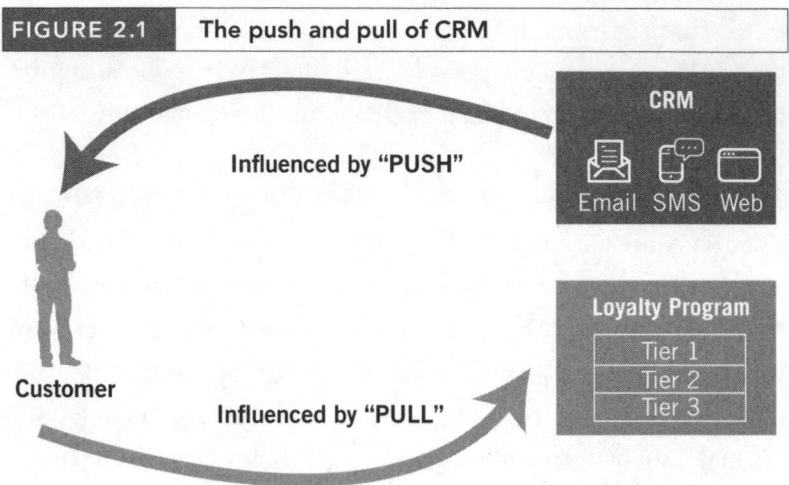

FIGURE 2.1   The push and pull of CRM

Rewards. Members relish collecting points, primarily on business trips, and using them for their vacations with family members. Attaining Executive Platinum and reaching the One Million Mile flight level are achievements that people are very proud of and talk about freely. However, I would argue that there is some waste in these programs and a very significant cost of the contingent liability of carrying those points on the balance sheet. Optimizing the expense and having shelf programs that drain miles effectively is critical. The plethora of external partners in many of these programs is overwhelming for members and as a result not valued since consumers only have so much mindshare.

Case Study: Starbucks Rewards

Starbucks made many changes to its rewards program in 2016, and the reactions expressed by Starbucks zealots on social media were quite amusing. Clearly the loyal drip coffee drinkers were not pleased that the change meant that it would take 2.5 times the spend on their regular brew to earn the same reward value before the change in the program.

This dramatic change highlights why it is so important to get the construct and economics of a loyalty program correct right out of the gate, as a substantial modification leads to a feeling of mistrust from customers and can have a negative impact on the morale of employees as they deal with the complaints. While many have lauded the Starbucks Rewards program since its launch in 2009, and I am sure Starbucks has been thrilled with the adoption of mobile payment, the economic challenges could have been predicted given the extreme frequency of the most loyal customers. And the operational issue of split transactions (people doing a transaction for each item to get more rewards) has been highlighted as one reason for the change, though that is secondary. In the casino vernacular I am familiar with, my thesis is the reinvestment rate of likely 16 percent in the old scheme was untenable from a profitability perspective going forward; therefore, Starbucks lowered it to 6.4 percent in essence, though there may be new ways to earn Stars that will increase that rate. The relative transparency of the program has enabled numerous publications and customers to do the math to see what type of customer is impacted and by how much. Starbucks is not the first company to make this kind of change; the airlines have changed their approach to incrementally reward higher fares and purchasing first-class seats that business travelers buy.

The old design of the Starbucks program violates some of the core loyalty principles we believe in at GALE as we help our clients conceive and modify their programs. The first principle is that it is best to tie the rewards amount to profitability. Second, as much of the marketing spend as possible should be surgical, tied to incremental spend and behaviors, as opposed to programmatic, associated with purchases the customer would have given you anyway. Finally, tiers that provide aspirational benefits, experiences, and services that customers value—in many cases more than points—are a critical component of a loyalty program, because if developed properly, the cost to deliver differentiated benefits will not be directly correlated to the spend the customer gives you. That is, tier benefits should be much more economically viable than points and will lead to even greater satisfaction from your best customers. In the Starbucks situation, think about a few critical things the company could do to personalize the experience for the customers it knows best—such as having your favorite drink ready at the time you come every day.

Developing a loyalty program that provides a strong value proposition to its customers and that is optimal for the company requires three essential components: a sophisticated modeling of current behavior and future spend and redemption patterns, a deep understanding of consumer behavior both with your firm and with the competitive set, and creativity as it relates to service benefits and rewards. Then once the nuanced mechanics are established, it is critical to spend significant time educating employees and customers about the value proposition so that they become advocates of the program and the brand more broadly. It's an extremely complicated exercise—but when it is done right, it can offer huge rewards both to customers and to the company's long-term strategic goals.

`01110100 11100100110000101011 11100111`
`11 00 100011 110111101101101010 101111`

Doubling Down

- **Service benefits are an economical way to add real value.** Creating compelling differentiated benefits and experiences is a very economical way to add value to a loyalty program and deepen relationships with customers.

- **It's better to add than to take away.** When rolling out a new or enhanced loyalty program, consider the notion of minimum viable product. Launch with a small number of meaningful components that you can execute and that customers can understand, but realize it is always better to add elements than it is to have to take them away.

- **Successful programs require rigorous financial analysis.** There must be rigor in the financial analysis to understand the economics of a new or enhanced loyalty scheme incorporating models of customer behavior and consumer feedback from research to ensure success and financial viability.

- **CRM and loyalty programs go hand in hand.** It is most powerful when companies have sophisticated CRM and a compelling loyalty program working in concert both for customers and for their business.

CHAPTER
3

The Evolution of Total Rewards

As we evolved Total Rewards over the years (see Figure 3.1), we considered the positive and negative dynamics of popular loyalty programs in our efforts to enhance the value proposition. When we started in 1998, there was only one tier in a program called Total Gold and focused primarily on slots players. The first thing we did was to add two tiers to the program, Platinum and Diamond, to create aspiration and engender more loyalty from our guests, as our research indicated we were only capturing 36 percent of their gaming budget. We wanted to give the customer a reason to be more loyal to us and not just visit whichever casino was offering them the best incentives that week. We also wanted to help our employees identify the best customers. Our employees treated VIPs with high spend on a daily trip very well, as is the custom in the industry, but the person who was coming 30+ times a year

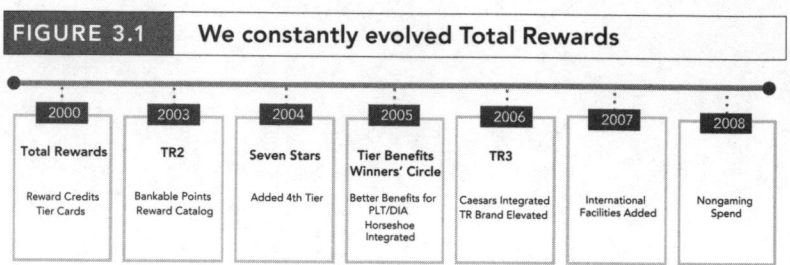

Tailored correctly, soft benefits drive significant Share of Wallet on (potentially) more profitable rewards especially when combined surgical and realtime CRM

and only spending $100 per trip was not receiving any special recognition and service. This significant paradigm shift for the industry, which we led, was to recognize customers for their annual value and not just daily spend level, which had been the sole way to identify a VIP since casino gambling began.

Establishing Consistent Criteria

To establish consistent tier criteria and benefits across the company was a significant challenge that required much debate and discussion, as our market dynamics and properties across the enterprise varied dramatically. We wanted to have uniform criteria we could communicate universally to customers and employees, but we also realized that the frequency of customer visitation, distribution of annual and daily spend level, and competitive dynamics varied by market pretty significantly, as did the ability to execute differentiated service benefits at each of our properties. We did detailed analyses to understand the concentration of visits on weekends and weekdays at various thresholds for the Diamond criteria and conducted operational management studies to determine how each property could handle peak times effectively. Ultimately, we arrived at a set of criteria that everyone

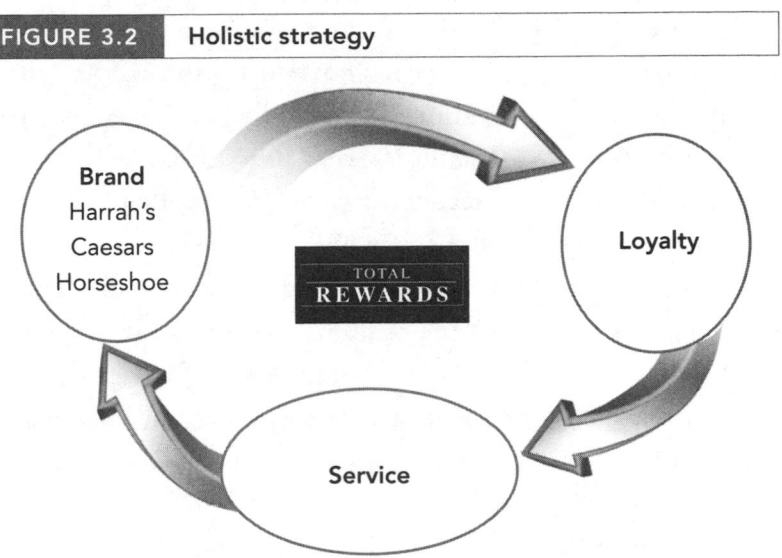

FIGURE 3.2   Holistic strategy

could live with and that we thought provided attainable goals for our customers to play up to, reducing their trips to our competitors. We renamed the program *Total Rewards* and launched the tiers to much success in 2000, as we saw that our share of the gaming budget for Diamond customers increased to 50 percent with the desire of customers to achieve that valuable status.

At this early stage of establishing Harrah's as an elite marketing and customer-centric organization, we had three main pillars upon which we were building our strategy: brand, loyalty, and customer service (see Figure 3.2). If a company can execute against all three of these well, it is going to outperform its competitors.

Creating a Bankable Currency

The next major enhancement we made to Total Rewards was also a significant change management exercise that required much debate and deep analytics over many months before we determined the path forward. We had several objectives in the initiative we called TR2, signifying the next generation of the program, even though Total Rewards had been consistently voted the best loyalty program in the casino industry and had started to receive significant recognition more broadly in publications such as the *Wall Street Journal* and *Harvard Business Review*.

The first goal was to create a bankable currency that customers could save up across multiple trips and use however they wanted. The historic model was based on what is called *discretionary comping*; this meant that the customer had to ask an employee for a food comp, and it was at the employee's discretion, with the assistance of some rules that were displayed in the Casino Management System, to choose what to offer primarily based on their daily spend level.

One of the primary challenges of this, in addition to the often awkward dialogue between an hourly employee and a guest, was that our very significant and valuable set of frequent but low-spending customers couldn't get much based on their daily worth—perhaps a latte or a discount to the buffet. This was very frustrating to the customers based on their cumulative spend over the course of the month and led to heated discussions forcing employees to acquiesce to the customers' demands of being able to have a nice dinner at a gourmet restaurant on a fairly regular basis. By allowing the customers to save what they earned on a daily basis over multiple trips in TR2, they were now free to have a great meal when they had earned enough Reward Credits (points) if that is what they chose. Or they could go to the buffet more frequently or save up for an item in our merchandise catalog or for their annual trip to Las Vegas. It was totally their choice to use the points whenever and wherever they wanted to at any of our properties.

We analyzed the $350 million of comp spend at the time and saw how unfairly it was being distributed to the most vocal customers. Our objective was to allocate at least 80 percent of that spend to a points-based system that customers could comprehend and have in their control; the other 20 percent would remain in a discretionary bucket for our casino hosts to use both for VIP customers who had abnormally large losses on a particular visit and for customers deemed to have upside potential.

Creating Portability

Another challenge we needed to fix was to provide portability of points for customers across our nationally distributed Total Rewards program. Access to multiple markets and brands was one of the things we touted quite a bit in our marketing collateral, but the reality is that there was a lot of friction for the customers in the process as they visited a new market. For example, suppose a customer who played often and was quite valuable to our St. Louis property had booked his annual trip to Las Vegas and planned to stay and play at one of our Vegas properties. Prior to TR2, upon arrival, the customer might ask to eat before playing, but he would be told by an employee that he had to play before he would be given a comp. Imagine that customer's frustration when he had played so much at a Total Rewards property throughout the year. Or the Las Vegas property could say yes and hope that their casino would actually see the play as opposed to the customer choosing to play at one of the glittering competitors on the Strip.

By creating a centralized bank, the customer would be able to eat or see shows using the points he had earned from all his visits in St. Louis; as well, the Vegas property was made whole by being paid out of the bank for the cost of the meal or show, so Vegas had every incentive to let the customer enjoy his dining or entertainment experience as they were being paid the retail rate as opposed to the hard cost of the meal. This portability was a huge satisfier to customers and led to a significant increase in cross-property play; in fact, more than half of our revenue came from customers playing at a property other than their most frequently visited one.

And analytically we were able to prove that customers who visited multiple properties in a market or across markets were significantly more valuable in both the short and long term.

Making the Program More Appealing

The final major objective of TR2 was to make the program more appealing to table game players and reduce the perception that the program was just a slots club. To continue to grow and with the success we were seeing in table games in New Orleans and Lake Tahoe, we felt it was important to embrace this group more fully in Total Rewards. We worked on clarifying how customers earned Rewards Credits based on their play and made it easier for play to be tracked by rolling out technology at each table game.

Perhaps the biggest debate we had in the process was whether to base the points-earning methodology on coin-in or whether it should be based on theoretical; believe me, there were some very heated discussions on this topic both within my team and with several key operators. The benefit of a coin-in approach is that it is easy for customers to understand and employees to explain, because for every dollar played through any game, there is a set amount of points earned. The downside is that the transparency makes it very difficult to make a change to the detriment of the customer without there being consequences. The benefit of a theoretically (theo) based program is that it is tied to profitability, as slot machines have dramatically different hold percentages by denomination, meaning $100 played on one game could be worth a lot less than it is on another machine. In addition, a theo-based system allows for a nonlinear reinvestment rate at a daily level; this allowed us to invest modestly for low-level customers, have a peak reinvestment rate for very good customers so they could enjoy a meal at one of our gourmet restaurants, and ramp it down a bit at the extreme high end where customers would otherwise earn more points than they could reasonably consume on a daily basis.

I and others fought hard for this, and fortunately we went with a theo-based program, as we were able to lower the earning rate in 2009 to save money after the economic crisis without the customers knowing it explicitly and penalizing us for it. To increase the customers' understanding of how they were earning, we showed them their balance right at the game, and they could check their balance at kiosks on property and on the Total Rewards website, and we eventually built a WAP site as customers were quite curious about their balance. We also made it very clear what they could get for the points with rewards menus throughout the property and on the website.

Once we determined what we were going to do, we spent a significant amount of time and energy on how we were going to communicate the program to customers and employees to get them excited about the changes. We genuinely felt like we were making the program better for customers; still, we knew that there would be skepticism about the changes, especially given that other well-known loyalty programs had made changes to the detriment of customers, most notably Delta Sky Miles that had generated negative customer sentiment.

The theme we used to describe the program was "MORE": more control for the customers, meaning they could use their comps for a broader variety of things than food—and could use them in more locations (see Figure 3.3). We supported the launch of TR2 with a national promotion that we called the 100 Million Reward Credit Giveaway with a broad set of prizes that were reflective of what was available in the program, including merchandise and experiences at our properties such as Jazz Fest in New Orleans or lift tickets at Heavenly in Lake Tahoe. The Reward Credit moniker was to help customers get a feel for what a

FIGURE 3.3   Total Rewards brand

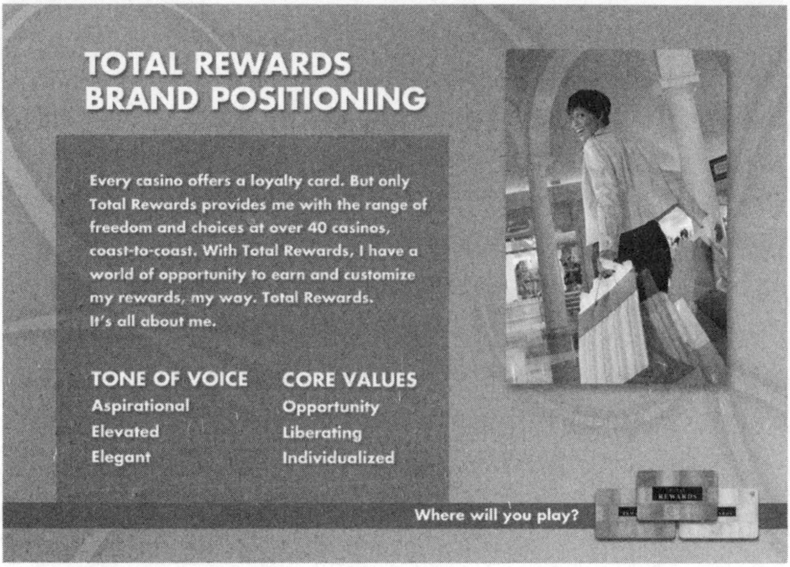

Reward Credit was worth generally speaking, though we had the ability to modulate that by market or for promotional purposes.

Finally, in the six weeks prior to the launch of TR2 on June 17, 2003, we had two groups doing employee rallies across all our properties day and night to help our frontline staff get excited about the program and sell it to the customers they talk to every day. We knew it was important to get the workers on board with the changes, as their opinion was very important to the customers who would be asking about what the changes meant for them.

Monitoring Customer Feedback and Implementing Improvements

TR2 was a major technology initiative as well, given how differently we were going to track, redeem, and account for comps in the new model. While some companies have the luxury of testing large changes in a market or two or have the ability to stage the rollout over several weeks, that wasn't the case for us. Because our customers visited multiple markets, often within a condensed period of time, we had to implement TR2 as an enterprise wide changeover. The collaboration between marketing, IT, and operations throughout the process paid off in a very stressful but successful day that had only a few minor hiccups.

TR2 generally was well received from the outset, but we were constantly monitoring customer performance and feedback to determine what if anything needed to be modified. Two interesting things came up analytically within the first couple of months that highlighted opportunities for improvement that we needed to address. The first is that we found that guest satisfaction with Total Rewards was much lower for those customers that had not yet redeemed any of their Reward Credits (RCs), the theory being that they had yet to have a positive experience with the program's new currency. To rectify this, we did a targeted communication to those customers who had a meaningful balance and had not redeemed their credits, suggesting a variety of things they could get with their current point balance.

The second thing we learned from our research was that there were two distinct groups within our VIP population as it related to comping meals to our restaurants. We labeled one group "Account Watchers," as the group's members were very interested in knowing in real time how many points they had and how their balance was reduced when they used their points for food or other things on the rewards menu. The people in this group wanted regular communication about where they stood with their RCs.

We labeled the other group "Take Care of Me," as the members of this group were not as concerned about the mechanics of the program and how many points they had; they were more intensely focused on their gaming experience as an escape from their everyday lives. When they were ready for a break and it was time to eat, they wanted their host to make it easy for them to use their comps in the restaurant even though they realized their RCs would be decremented.

Leveraging this insight about the two groups, we created a video explaining the dynamics and highlighting the clues to look for so our hosts could take even better care of our best customers.

Developing Ultra-exclusivity

The next big change we made to Total Rewards was to add the Seven Stars tier in mid-2004, which I had pitched to CEO Gary Loveman and the management team on a couple of prior occasions unsuccessfully. There were several reasons that led us to want to add a tier at the extreme high end of our customer distribution. First, we discovered that we were capturing only a 50 percent share from our Diamond customers, as many of them were trying to achieve the equivalent tier at a competitor much like a business traveler in some markets tries to achieve status in two airline programs to provide more choices to be upgraded when flying. We wanted to make the decision more difficult to try to attain a high status at a competitor.

Second, we found that for our top 5,000 out of 10 million customers, there was significant revenue churn year to year at an individual level. That is one year a customer would spend $85,000 and the next $70,000. Given that this group was spending or losing $80,000 a year with us, a 20+ percent revenue drop from a quarter of them was significant. We realized that some of this drop was a matter of having less time or disposable income to gamble in a given year, but we also felt that a big reason for the variation year to year was that there was no transparent goal to attain.

Finally, these customers also expressed frustration that the benefits and amenities they received across the system were quite inconsistent. As an example, they didn't understand why they would receive a nice welcome basket in one market and not in another.

So we embarked on our journey to develop an ultra-exclusive tier for our top customers. Of course, there was much debate about the criteria and the benefits—and we even agreed about whether there was a reason to do it—but eventually we got consensus to move forward. We agreed to several core benefits that all properties would execute, and we allowed the properties to have their own benefits as well. We decided to call the tier Seven Stars because there were seven stars in the Harrah's logo; Bill Harrah was married seven times, and we felt like there was a positive connotation to the name. Another critical decision at the outset was that we decided to make the service delivery and communication covert, not having clear signage to identify different lines as we did for Diamond and Platinum. One of the reasons we did this was that we were concerned about upsetting our Diamond customers, whom we had put on a pedestal for the previous four years. Initially, there were just under 4,000 customers in Seven Stars, who collectively spent more than $250 million a year, and our motto was "The answer is yes, what would you like?"

We saw great success with Seven Stars as the tier grew and the revenue retention goal was met effectively. However, we did see that executing the differentiated service with the covert approach was quite challenging for customers and employees because it wasn't clear where to go for the service or easy to have an employee ready to handle this level of guest instantaneously. We had a lot more leverage with the initial doubters, given the program's success, to take a harder stand on several items that we had compromised on at the outset.

The first change was that we were going to become more public about the tier, adding signage on property to identify where to get the differentiated service and highlighting the tier in marketing collateral to create aspiration from high-level Diamonds to consolidate play with us. We knew that this would improve the service delivery, but we wanted to make sure we wouldn't alienate our Diamond customers in the process, so we ran focus groups to discuss it with them. Their feedback was that they knew there was another level of customer that deserved even a higher level of service and that they were fine with Seven Stars, assuming we weren't taking away Diamond tier benefits.

The next big change was to add to the enterprise wide benefits so that there would be even more consistency in the experience, as our best customers traveled across markets either of their own volition or by responding to our VIP event invitations. We still heard complaints from some of our Vegas operators about having to provide certain amenities to customers they saw from other markets once a year, especially when it was a lower-daily-value customer. We reiterated that there was no such thing as a bad Seven Stars customer given their spend level and that it was required that customers get the same treatment across all markets.

Another exercise we went through was to examine the proliferation of property-specific benefits that the operators had put in place to please these guests. A group of us locked ourselves in a room for a couple of days and discovered that there were more than 300 property-specific benefits. We determined that several should be consistently executed across the company; that others were worthy of being a Seven Starts tier benefit even if no other market could execute them, such as lift tickets at Heavenly or being on a float at Mardi Gras; and that still others were too down market for the tier to be published as a benefit, such as the milkshake one of the properties had on its list. If properties wanted to surprise their customers with a milkshake, more power to them—it just could not be listed as a benefit.

In addition to the enhancements to Seven Stars and the decision to publicize it, we decided that we would execute several signature Seven Stars events each year, whether that was creating a new event or leveraging things that we were already doing for top VIPs anyway. These included producing a great event around Jazz Fest in New Orleans and hosting Celebrity Golf in Lake Tahoe, and we developed memorable weekends in Las Vegas, Atlantic City, and other markets with gourmet meals, shopping, and fantastic entertainers. We elevated the collateral for Seven Stars and managed the communication centrally through my VIP team to ensure that everything these customers received was top-notch. With the acquisition of Horseshoe and Caesars relatively simultaneous to this change, Seven Stars grew to include more than 16,000 customers who spent more than $1 billion a year collectively.

Recognizing Nongaming Spend

The final major change we made to Total Rewards in my time at Harrah's and Caesars was to recognize nongaming spend to make the program relevant to an increasingly important group of customers who weren't necessarily big gamers but spent significant money on rooms, dining, shopping, entertainment, spa services, or golf. This was the most challenging project to get support for in all my time at Harrah's, as the Vegas operators argued that we were already getting more than $1 billion in nongaming revenue without incenting it through points. The counterargument was that we were not getting our fair share of nongaming spend in Vegas and Atlantic City partially because of superior assets and entertainment offerings from our competitors. We felt that an effective loyalty scheme would be another tool in our arsenal to convince customers to be more loyal and would enable us to learn more about both gaming and nongaming customers to further personalize our communication strategy with them. There was much debate about earning rates, and we settled on a 1 percent reward; it was common enough in co-branded credit card programs to be accepted by customers and a reasonable financial exposure for us. We launched just after the economic crisis, though, so the success was more modest than we had hoped for, but it still enabled us to grow nongaming revenue and have a program that had some relevance to a broader set of consumers.

While I provided a lot of specific detail about how Total Rewards evolved, my hope is that there are several critical transferable lessons. The first is that even despite the program's recognition as the best in the industry, we didn't sit back and rest on our laurels, but rather we continually enhanced the program. These changes were driven by deep analytic insights that spurred creative thinking that was informed by customer research and operator feedback to ensure that the customer was at the core of the design. Understanding the trade-offs between transparency and complexity is also critical to developing the right construct. Finally, there cannot be too much communication with employees and customers to ensure that everyone understands and values the program to maximize adoption and utilization.

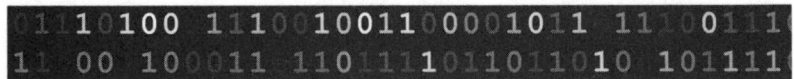

Doubling Down

- **Tiers create aspiration and engender loyalty.**
  Compelling tiers are a productive way to create aspiration from customers and have them give you more share of their spend in your category.

- **Tiers must be meaningfully differentiated.** Having meaningful differences in the benefits and services between tiers is critical. The thresholds should be determined by a robust analysis of your customer database. Having meaningful differences in benefits by tier helps inform how many tiers you should have.

- **Make the program frictionless for your customers.** It is critical to eliminate friction in the customer experience when customers interact with your loyalty program. It should be easy for them to use your currency *whenever* and *wherever* they want.

- **Don't stop innovating.** I can't emphasize this enough. Despite our many accolades, we at Caesars never stopped evolving, testing, and tinkering with Total Rewards, making it great for customers, but also for us.

Innovative Loyalty Design in Other Industries

Tremendous Opportunity Across Industries

I have long felt that the things we accomplished at Harrah's were applicable to a wide range of other industries, as we had many well-known companies come spend the day with us to talk and learn about loyalty, and I have certainly seen it in recent years on the consulting side. Clearly there are several key inherent advantages in the gaming industry to facilitate loyalty, including player cards that customers use to have their gaming activity tracked to get comps, the frequency with which customers come to casinos in most geographic locations, the amenities and services available to offer as rewards and incentives, and the scale of the business. However, the principles apply in many different verticals.

One industry where loyalty is applicable is retail, where there is a heavy product focus but not a customer-centric one beyond the objective to deliver great customer service to everyone in some examples. Merchants still have extreme power in retail organizations and often dictate marketing strategy, with the marketing team serving as merely executors. The primary communication objective is based on moving new or distressed product by targeting the whole customer base with the same message without regard to what is most appropriate for the customer.

It is common for retailers to talk about "omnichannel," but what does that really mean? Is it continuity from a channel perspective, operationally meaning that you can order from the store and receive your order at home or vice versa? Is it being able to fulfill from a common inventory system? These things are important and benefit the customer, but they are merely scratching the surface of what customer centricity means. Being able to truly understand the customer and present relevant content at the right moment through the right channel is the holy grail for which companies should strive in order to engender deep loyalty from customers. Data and technology can enhance the customer experience while simultaneously driving incremental profits for the company. Omnichannel should be about having continuity among all customer touchpoints and having one interaction build upon the previous one to get a more relevant and timely view. We have seen major retailers like Macy's shutter hundreds of stores and lay off thousands of employees as traffic to the physical stores decreases and customers move online, and this occurs without Macy's and others being able to maintain revenue and loyalty across channels. I am sure you have seen various iterations of the graphic shown in Figure 4.1 as people describe omnichannel.

FIGURE 4.1	Omnichannel approach

**Marketing Technology Ecosystem:
Improve Capabilities and Drive Quantifiable Results**

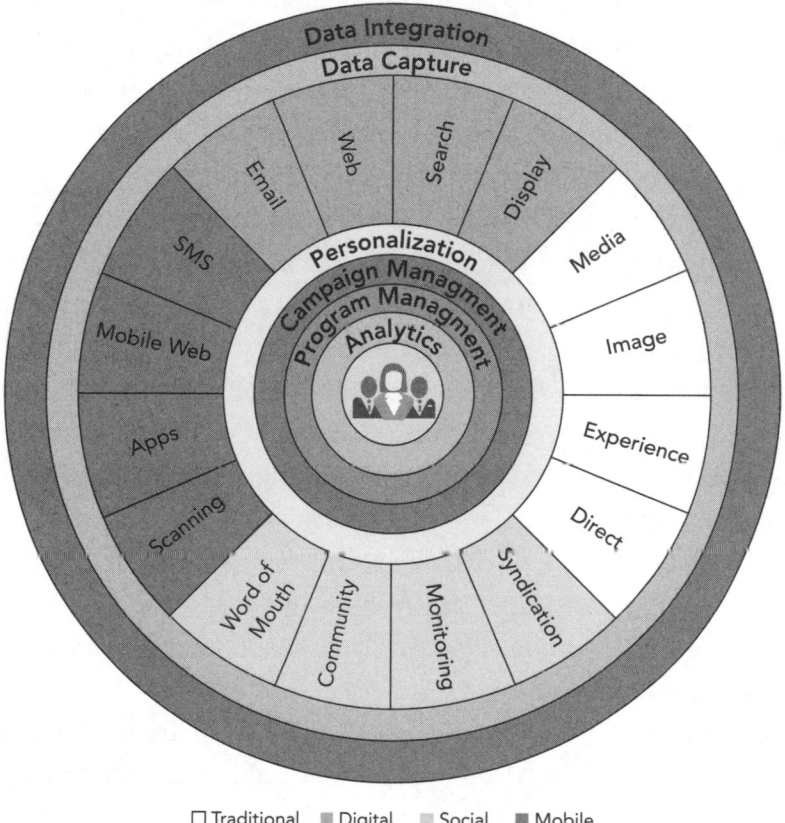

☐ Traditional   ▪ Digital   ▪ Social   ▪ Mobile

Informed and Elegant Approaches

For a loyalty program provider focused on the appeal of shopping locally, we conducted a deep analytics engagement, and what we found reinforced the idea that there are several critical elements to compelling programs. There has to be an everyday component on the earning side; we saw in our analysis that their most successful markets were those where they had grocery stores and gas stations at a higher rate than underperforming markets. People want to earn points for their necessary, nondiscretionary spend. We also saw that the most successful markets had a wide range of redemption options giving the customer flexibility to get a practical or aspirational item.

For a well-known retailer, we investigated an omnichannel approach starting with focus groups of customers and store associates. We began by asking them what they felt about the service in the store across the brand, and the general consensus was that the service was above average, with the group participants typically ranking the company in the 8-to-10 range on a 10-point scale. When we probed the participants on why they felt that way, they said because employees generally left them alone when they were in the store, which was true based on our observation as well; the associates kept busy by folding clothes and making modest rearrangements of merchandise.

We asked them how that perception would change if an associate was informed of what the customers had been exploring online and had previously purchased, enabling the associate to deliver a more personalized experience. The feedback was very positive from both sets of constituents, especially for certain shopping occasions where the customers did not typically shop the brand because of the relative complexity of the shopping experience given the diverse product mix. The customers felt the employee's having access to their individual profiles would allow the associate to truly find the right product for them based on their style, even if it was stretching their style comfort zone without going too far. One of the concerns people expressed was their own lack of confidence in being able to put an outfit together, and they felt this was a productive and nonintrusive way to do so and make sure that the outfit truly matched and hung together.

The associates felt like the technology driven solution would automate what they already did manually, allowing them to service more customers and to ensure their customers would get better service when they were not there or if a customer was traveling to another market. We followed the focus groups with quantitative research to help build the case internally. We knew that in addition to the explosive rate of the e-commerce business, people were exploring online before planning a visit to the store, but we were surprised by the magnitude of it. The most popular idea tested in both research forums was to be able to set an appointment where the fitting room would be curated with products from your wish list and complementary items to make the shopping experience both personalized and efficient. This reinforced the notion that people are often time constrained with all their day-to-day responsibilities and use mobile and digital to plan their in-store trips.

For a popular retailer we worked with, we focused on a deep microclustering exercise to help identify the opportunity to drive more revenue at a refined customer segment level based on multiple factors, including categories where customers had purchased from both a depth and breadth perspective, purchase channels, participation in the company's outdoor adventure program, and several other factors. The clustering work reinforced the idea that having continuity across multiple channels is a significant opportunity for companies to build deeper relationships with their customers. In this example, imagine the scenario where the consumer is exploring a big-ticket item online but wants to be able to visually compare a couple of options in store because it is such a significant, long-term investment. How great would it be if you could schedule an appointment to visit the store, and the associate was ready and waiting with all the relevant information about a range of product options to help you make the best decision?

Vail Resorts Case Study

Vail Resorts is a great example of this, under the leadership of CEO Rob Katz. He had the foresight and fortitude to invest in the infrastructure required to deploy Epic Mix, which tracks your skiing behavior and your resort activity. In addition to investing in the technology capital, Rob invested in the human capital required, starting with Bob Brown, who ran my marketing analysis team so well. Bob brought in some other folks from the team over time, and the combination of what they had learned at Harrah's and Caesars with the vision from Rob Katz has led to pure magic for Vail Resorts.

I met Rob in 2010 because of our common connection with Apollo and was able to ski with him on several occasions in Vail. In addition to enjoying one of the most beautiful and expansive ski resorts in the world, it was great to watch Rob interact with guests and hear about his vision of how he was going to further personalize the experience by taking advantage of technology and using data effectively. He had recently launched the Epic Mix, which tracked customers' behavior on the mountain via RFID technology. For the skier, it is fun to see how many vertical feet you have skied and how many trails you have experienced. For Vail, it provided a wealth of information and a value proposition to communicate with the customers.

After I left Caesars and talked to Rob about the type of resources he needed to bring his vision to life, I introduced him to Bob Brown, who had done such a great job on my team. I knew Bob was the perfect guy to analyze the emerging Vail data and turn his findings into insights and action. Bob subsequently recruited another half-dozen Caesars alums to replicate our successes at Vail.

With the Epic Mix, Vail locks in skiers with an annual pass at the start of the season, minimizing the risk of a bad snow season and securing revenue in November. Vail is using the data captured to personalize communication with customers across multiple channels, including mobile and in room, to encourage customers to book hotel rooms, make dining reservations, and buy ski gear. Vail has replicated other amenities and concierge experiences from the casino industry, including high-end clubs mid-mountain that offer excellent dining and a chance to warm up.

The Vail Resorts example shows how a visionary CEO and a talented team can achieve great results very quickly to improve the customer experience and company profitability. When you visit any of Vail's properties around the world, you will receive a highly personalized experience.

Financial Services, Healthcare, and Other Areas of Opportunity

There is a significant opportunity to create a more customer-centric approach in financial services, as product silos still dominate communication with customers. Rarely is there a chief customer officer at large financial institutions, and if there is, the officer's authority isn't significant enough to drive a more cohesive customer-oriented approach. Each product unit targets its customers without a lot of insight into the value of other products and without regard for having a coordinated communication stream for clients.

At GALE, we are helping several financial services companies do very progressive things using data and technology to drive a more personalized experience across multiple touchpoints.

Financial services companies are starting to adopt big data and digital technology more effectively to drive value through cross-selling and upselling by enabling branch office employees to have a much more personalized and relevant interaction with customers when they are in the branch. Based on the products the customer already has and the customer's detailed profile, recommendations are provided to the associate on what to offer the customer in real time as the salesperson talks to the customer. This is a great example of the power of integrating big data analytics with digital technology to create a win for both the customer and the company. Banks have seen a meaningful lift in the number of expanded relationships acquired in their branches.

Financial institutions that are focused on the investment side of the business can also build a data-driven process to generate more effective leads by matching the profile of the advisors and investors. Sales personnel can be provided with prioritized investor leads to maximize their time, and it provides managers with more insight about how individuals on their team are penetrating their sales leads. Recommended actions and comprehensive contextual information to enrich the quality of the sales conversations should also be provided to ensure the right discussion is taking place and to allow sales personnel to focus their effort on the best opportunities available, leading to improved sales conversions.

There is an opportunity in pet care and healthcare as well, as demonstrated by the work at National Veterinary Associates (NVA). Imagine if your local animal hospital reached out proactively with relevant content based on the breed of dog you have. By putting in Carol Henry, who had worked with me at Harrah's, as the CMO and with the support of the CEO Greg Hartmann,

NVA has been able to do segmented marketing for its hospitals for several years now. More recently NVA has pushed the next wave of sophistication in its targeted marketing by building new capabilities that further customize the interactions with pet owners and increase the measurability of marketing activities.

There is also an opportunity to improve personalization in human healthcare. The industry is very product focused with a heavy emphasis on general advertising, and there is hardly any patient-centric communication. Relevant messaging about preventative medicine and other info would make a big difference and likely would be a more efficient use of marketing dollars than all the TV spots and direct mail that are used today. It seems like healthcare is starting to make progress in this area, but it is still very early.

There are many incredible resorts around the world that provide a fabulous service experience where a guest feels special and pampered. However, rarely is that service driven by a deep knowledge of who you are, partially justified in the resort world because many of the guests are once-in-a-lifetime visitors. However, for other hotel brands that capture some degree of visitation because of having a diverse array of locations, there is more opportunity to personalize the experience across a multitude of touchpoints. When was the last time you had your favorite beverage waiting for you in the in-room refrigerator or your preferred snack was sitting on the table? When was the last time you received a highly personalized email or direct mail piece or content on a hotel website about returning to a special destination or introducing you to the next perfect place to go?

I believe second-stage start-ups have a significant opportunity to use data to personalize the experience and stimulate the next wave of growth. Often these businesses have developed around a product or technology, with the consumer being secondary in the organization's orientation based on the founders' skills and interest. Acquisition and the number of users or customers are often the primary objectives to secure additional funding, but building the tools to drive repeat purchases can make for a sustainable and growing business.

There is also a tremendous opportunity to add customer-centric capabilities to private equity owned firms. Many private equity firms have owned a significant portion of their portfolio companies for several years, and much of the cost cutting and operational efficiency work has been done. To create an interesting story for a successful exit, building out marketing capabilities to drive revenue is a tactic that can and should be employed much more often. With several of the Summit Partners businesses I have been affiliated with as a board member, we have seen success by adding a marketing-centric approach to complement a successful operationally driven one. This combination of operational and marketing excellence has led to impressive same-store sales growth, which has led to highly lucrative exits.

There is even an opportunity in consumer packaged goods companies (CPGs), even though they often don't know much about their customers generally, given that they sell most of their product indirectly through retail stores. Historically most of the marketing expense has been dedicated to in-store promotions to secure the best shelf space, and a fraction of that budget has been dedicated to true marketing. There has been a hesitation to build direct to consumer revenue-generating websites lest the CPGs alienate the retailers who sell their products. Furthermore, within CPGs, each of the brands typically operates independently, managing its P&L and marketing activities on its own.

Our vision for CPGs is to create a relationship with customers so that we can better know their interests and buying behaviors and so that we can provide meaningful content as well as cross-sell products within and across brands. The first step is to create a relevant content site that drives repeat traffic to the site and creates a reason and mechanism to know the customer directly.

It is critical to achieve several technical objectives in building the site, including being able to track what content the consumers are engaging with so that we can personalize what they see when they come to the site the next time. We also have the intention to build this initial infrastructure on a platform that can scale up to support all the company's brands over time, as that would facilitate our knowing the consumer across all the businesses under the company's umbrella.

To attract the brands to the idea of working with us, we start with a very beautiful website with amazing photography and content to complement our business strategy. Many of the CPGs' brands have asked us to build websites for them that not only help them drive brand loyalty and commerce, but support the goal of knowing the customer across organizational silos.

Knowing the customer enables us to do sophisticated CRM activities, which can drive direct purchases for the CPG, especially if it builds enhanced fulfillment capabilities. This is another way for the various brands to connect with customers directly and increase relevance in their everyday activities.

Amazon's recent deal to acquire Whole Foods is the ultimate example of bringing this notion to life. The combination of Amazon's ability to understand customers and drive personalization with Whole Foods' physical locations and supply chain capabilities will be extremely powerful as Amazon penetrates the grocery space.

Price Sensitivity

We have been able to use our Ask GALE research panel to do several price-sensitivity testing exercises across a variety of industries. As companies struggle to grow, they often wonder how a change in pricing strategy will affect their business from a demand perspective. If they raise prices, how much demand will go away? If they lower prices, will they be able to stimulate enough incremental sales to offset the lower prices on revenue they would have gotten at the higher price?

We have done this work primarily in what would be defined as luxury and discretionary spending categories, ranging from a product that had been in the market for a long time but was now deemed too expensive compared with competitors to a proposed start-up that conceived a new solution to our age old problem. We have also done it in the healthcare space, in one instance seeing how much more demand there was if the company added a slightly lower price point and in another seeing how much more could be charged without threatening demand.

We typically start our diagnosis with an Ask GALE survey to understand customers' purchase intentions in the category and their view of various brands. Through the research, we develop a product innovation road map based on consumers' interest in our client's product and their view on alternatives. We identify areas to reclaim and innovate, and we are also on the lookout for further threats from the competition.

In our research, we work to understand price curves to determine the optimal price point to maximize profit, balancing the view of the product being seen as too expensive to consider or too inexpensive to reflect a quality product. How best to bundle services and benefits is often a key part of the elegance of finding the right answer on the pricing curve. Our model determines at a high level, both the best price to drive the optimal profit for the brand and the best way to communicate to customers to drive higher price points, which can lead to an even more sophisticated pricing analysis or a test in market.

Keeping track of metrics and evolving rewards programs based on implicit and explicit customer feedback are key to a program's success. At GALE we have pushed this approach even further based on our big data capabilities and have helped numerous clients across a range of industries develop new programs or modify existing ones to transform the trajectory of our clients' businesses with an innovative approach to their loyalty schemes.

Doubling Down

- **Go top-down and bottom-up.** When implementing a new program or changing an existing one, it is imperative to get support both top-down from the Executive team and bottom-up with frontline employees to ensure success.

- **Leverage your unique assets.** Leverage the unique assets of your business when creating a loyalty program to create meaningful differentiated benefits and service experiences or different price point to vary levels.

- **Have a diverse set of KPIs.** Have several key metrics regarding your loyalty program that you can effectively measure to determine how engaged your customers are.

- **Multiple ways to create a value proposition.** Given if loyalty mechanisms are not standard in your industry, a win-win value proposition can be established with your customers.

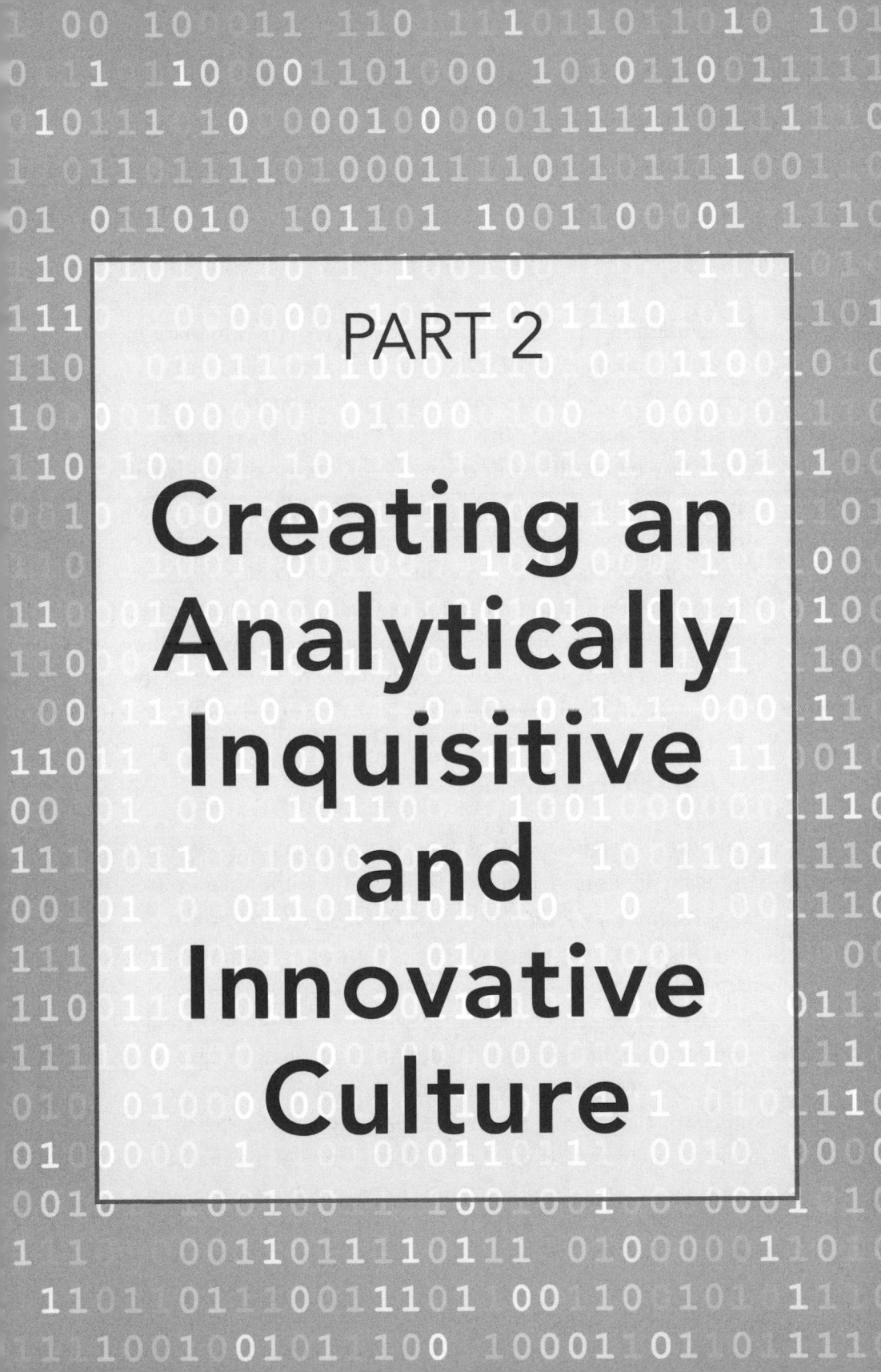

PART 2

Creating an Analytically Inquisitive and Innovative Culture

In addition to having the right tools and resources in place to conduct sophisticated analysis quickly, companies must also create a culture where insights supersede intuition and constant evolution is embraced. This starts with a top-down approach where fact-based, data-informed arguments are demanded as opposed to putting more weight on opinions. While a balance of art and science in decision making is necessary, the latter should be the dominant factor. The most successful companies are able to take data-driven insights and make rapid decisions, whether that is implementing a short-term modification to everyday activities or making a strategic pivot to take advantage of an opportunity.

Approach to Analytics

Clearly there has been a lot of focus on analytics in recent years, and many firms have invested significantly both in data warehouse technology and in people in order to try to know more about their business. The challenge I continue to see is that companies have large stacks of reports but don't genuinely garner the insights they need from their analytic process to be able to make more rapid and informed decisions. An important principle is to be able to get insights in summary form at a glance in order to understand at a high level what is happening, then be able to peel back the onion and get a deeper understanding of the challenges and opportunities. Similar to the philosophy on queries, automating the execution of standard reports, as opposed to doing

FIGURE P2.1	A customer-centric and analytic approach should have wide implications across an organization

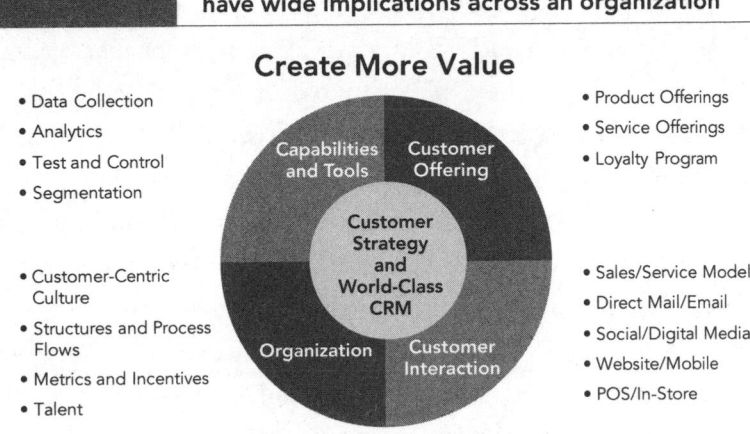

Create More Value

- Data Collection
- Analytics
- Test and Control
- Segmentation

- Customer-Centric Culture
- Structures and Process Flows
- Metrics and Incentives
- Talent

Capabilities and Tools

Customer Offering

Customer Strategy and World-Class CRM

Organization

Customer Interaction

- Product Offerings
- Service Offerings
- Loyalty Program

- Sales/Service Model
- Direct Mail/Email
- Social/Digital Media
- Website/Mobile
- POS/In-Store

Capture More Value

Excel jockeying just to get the required reports produced, is critical in order to free up the analytic resources to spend more time creating insights for decision makers.

Ultimately a customer-centric and analytic-driven approach should have wide implications across the organization (see Figure P2.1).

The best thing we did in my time at Harrah's to improve our analytic insights was to create the Marketing Analysis Managers (MAM) group in 2003. We had automated dozens of standard reports that were helpful in understanding customer and business performance easily and quickly in order to make informed decisions. However, when there was a special analytic need, sometimes the properties were challenged to do extremely sophisticated work in a timely fashion based on the resources available to them locally. To improve that, we created the MAM group, which consisted typically of MBAs who were analytically inquisitive but also had strong communication skills. We had six of them and spread them geographically so that they could be close to the four to five properties that they each supported. This proximity enabled them to be pulled into meetings easily by general managers and VPs of marketing at the property level.

Also, given that they were situated on property, they were viewed much less like a corporate resource even though that is where they reported. As a result the MAMs were able to build great personal and professional relationships with the local teams.

The other critical thing was that their jobs were to do more complex, unique analysis, and they didn't have day-to-day executional responsibilities that would be prioritized over this work. This talented group enabled us to create detailed insights that we could turn into a surgical marketing response very quickly to rebuild revenue and eliminate ineffective marketing spend. The people in the group became such trusted partners with the operators that after a year or two, they were recruited to be property VPs of marketing or finance, which helped upgrade the talent in the field.

I have seen numerous large companies create centralized analytics functions as their solution to improve the insights to drive the business. While there are advantages of having a large group of like-minded people working together to share knowledge, techniques, and best practices, I have also seen disadvantages.

First, in large organizations like major financial institutions, given the scale of the companies, the centralized analytics groups by necessity become quite large and difficult to manage. Often these groups are led by someone whose career trajectory has been the result of analytic acumen, and it becomes very challenging for the person to manage a team of this scale while being able to keep a hand in the work that he or she is skilled at and loves.

There is a balance required of having narrow expertise by the analyst in a particular business function with giving analysts an opportunity to develop their skills by working on multiple business units. This conflict is a significant challenge.

Finally, prioritizing work across business units often leads to the biggest difficulty, as each brand or product line wants its analysis as quickly as possible. Frustration occurs when there isn't timely delivery, and the business units may hire their own analytic resource to be in better control of their destiny.

Even within my own team at Harrah's, I didn't centralize analysis, as I wanted each of my direct reports and their functional areas to be able to drive the insights they needed quickly in order to make changes. Even though there would have been some logic to creating a shared service analytic group, either under the group of statisticians in the capability development area or under the MAMs, I resisted that temptation. I wanted my vice president, Monica Sullivan, who had responsibility for digital advertising and traditional media to be able to optimize spend by channel, market, and brand based on what she was seeing to maximize room nights and visitation. Similarly, I wanted my vice president of VIP, Brett Kline, to be able to provide analytics from the player contact system to the field in near real time with resources that were under his control.

In early 2009 we decided to centralize all marketing analysis for the properties under the MAM group, as we needed to be more effective with our marketing spend in the aftermath of the economic crisis. This required disciplined decisions based on sophisticated analysis, which in turn was based on understanding the incrementality of each marketing program at a customer level. When I proposed this to the three division presidents and senior management team, consensus was reached in a matter of seconds because they had so much respect for what we had accomplished with the MAM group over the previous six years. Not only had this group been a valued partner to the operators, but many MAM alums had taken on important property roles. This was the easiest change management activity I had ever proposed, even though understanding marketing performance was critical to the property success, as nearly half the revenue could be tied back to a proactive marketing incentive we had sent to the customer. All that the operators asked was to make sure we resourced the group sufficiently to provide timely analysis. We added junior analysts under the MAMs, which both provided them with a management opportunity and helped provide career progression for the junior analysts. This change dramatically improved our marketing effectiveness and was deemed a significant success.

In early 2011, the decision was made to centralize all analysis under the CFO; reporting to a talented person in the CFO's organization who had developed some great reporting capabilities and run revenue management for our Las Vegas properties. There was not much discussion allowed on this subject at an executive level, as it was presented as a fait accompli to the senior management team. Many of us felt like this took centralization too far, separating all analytic resources from the operators and creating a group that was going to be too large in scale to be manageable. When groups like this are created, there is a need for a lot of process with service-level agreements, submission forms, prioritization committees, and other time-consuming bureaucracy. This decision and outcome was one of the primary reasons I decided to leave Caesars, as I thought it was both a bad outcome and a bad process and disrupted one of the best marketing analytic functions in the world. In addition, a senior management group that had spent a lot of time and money to become more cohesive and an effective sounding board for the CEO was fractured by the rogue process of a few.

In this section, we will discuss the talent, structure, processes, and lessons learned in how to create an analytically driven organization where facts outweigh opinions and science dominates art. In addition to more common analysis, we will talk about measuring customer service and brand health and the critical implications of modifying a business when insights can be turned into action quickly.

Organizational Dynamics

Successfully ingraining a customer-centric orientation within a company requires a number of organizational dynamics to be in place. These range from top-down support and push from the CEO to bottom-up training of frontline employees. Inefficiency in organizational processes at the very least leads to delays in capturing the value possible, and at the worst it leads to turnover among key personnel.

Having a CEO that supports CRM and loyalty initiatives is an important ingredient, as the CEO helps overcome obstacles that may arise across the enterprise, including lack of funding from the CFO or poor buy-in from the field. While any CEO knows a strong customer orientation is paramount, in a surprisingly large number of instances that approach is only focused on customer service and not on a broader customer-centric orientation. Particularly in retail, CEOs tend to have come up through the merchandise track and have a tremendous product expertise, but they don't push for the leading-edge capabilities around the knowledge of the customer at an individual level.

At Caesars, the CEO Gary Loveman was passionate about customizing all our guest interactions, and this orientation and his mandate definitely helped drive adoption throughout the organization. He was willing to invest significantly in human and technology capital to ensure we had the resources to be world class in this area. His ambitions also placed a healthy pressure on my team and me to constantly evolve our capabilities and get more refined with our approach over time.

Establishing Senior-Level Committees

While less critical than internal buy-in, having a board of directors that is in support of building these capabilities is a positive as well and the directors can help challenge whether the appropriate talent is in place to execute the agenda. They must also have the right amount of patience to realize that an investment is required and that lower revenue or higher costs may result in the early stages of creating a learning culture and orientation.

As an aside, in my time at Harrah's and Caesars, I worked in both a public and private equity board setting, and I much preferred the latter. While both situations have very impressive and smart people, the meeting dynamics of the private board were much more engaging and interactive, leading to meatier discussions. The board members were also more helpful in overcoming organizational barriers that might exist to get new things done and would drive to action. I have had the pleasure of serving on three boards with Craig Frances of Summit Partners, two of which have had very successful exits, and I am sure the third one will as well. I appreciate the approach Summit takes with its portfolio companies by providing tremendous support and intellectual horsepower and pushing the companies to an even higher level of greatness in a highly collaborative way.

While everyone was inundated with meetings at Harrah's, establishing senior-level committees—one called the Operations Committee and the other the Marketing Council—was a critical element in our successful implementation of so many projects for several reasons. The Operations Committee would meet for a couple of days a quarter initially level set business performance so there would be context around where new capabilities were most needed. We would then dive into the specifics of the new initiatives, aided by but not beholden to PowerPoint, in order to drive debate and discussion to ensure all possibilities were considered to get to the best outcome. Once we determined as a group what we were going to do, we maintained alignment with limited back-channeling to the CEO to provide a united front to the rest of the organization as we communicated with our respective teams.

The Marketing Council brought together the top corporate and field marketers to discuss and debate a wide range of topics both tactical and strategic, from new brand campaigns to CRM capabilities. Chaired by the CEO, the Marketing Council was another forum in which to debate and discuss new initiatives from a wide range of perspectives to get to the best outcome. Once agreement was reached, we would maintain a unified front between corporate and the field as we drove toward implementation throughout the organization. For many years we supplemented the Marketing Council meetings with a several-day Marketing Summit for the top hundred or so marketers from across the company. In addition to internal content, we had external speakers from top companies or other areas of interest to help push our collective thinking well beyond the casino world, and several times we held the summits in compelling locations such as Disney World and the Fairmont in Banff so we could also learn from the customer experience that top resorts provide their guests.

Strong Functional Task Forces Are Critical to Success

We found that putting together strong cross-functional task forces was absolutely critical to our success for big initiatives. We made sure we had a broad array of talented people, representing different functions and regions of the operation and including a good mix of corporate and field people. This ensured that we explored issues from all angles, including markets with diverse competitive dynamics, to get to the best solution. In addition, this helped with organizational buy-in, as the recommendations were from the collective group and not thrown over from the ivory tower of the corporate team. These task forces started with a couple-day session where the corporate team would present as much data as possible so the group members were as informed as they could be. We would then brainstorm solutions without constraining ourselves unnecessarily at the outset before determining a road map with multiple releases prioritized on value and feasibility of implementation. We would then break into work teams that would push the thinking forward on particular topics within the project until the next group meeting. Our most challenging projects were tackled through this process and consistently led to great results.

Developing Joint Accountability

One of the consistent challenges I have seen at the companies that are struggling to implement customer-centric capabilities is that the CMO and their team are nearly entirely focused on near-term activities and short-term results and aren't allowed to focus enough thought and energy on longer-term actions. Understandably the CMO must balance the time appropriately, given company circumstances, on both the short and long term. But within the team, having some people completely dedicated to one or the other is an important step, as without a disciplined structure the bias will always divert resources to near-term results.

The relationship between the CMO and CIO is absolutely critical to the success of the enterprise. Developing a close partnership and joint accountability for the success of projects drives tremendous results and permeates both of the executives' teams and limits the typical finger-pointing that can occur—the marketing folks blaming IT for delays and defects, and IT accusing the marketers of scope creep. It is important the CMO and CIO be aligned on the priorities and determine which projects will be pursued. Visiting executives were always amazed at the partnership between Tim Stanley and me. In addition to spending a lot of time together at work conceiving projects and solutions, we spent time together skiing. When Tim left to pursue other more entrepreneurial activities, I encouraged the CEO to promote one of my direct reports, Katrina Lane, who had been involved in a significant number of IT projects, to become the CIO. While there was some initial resistance to that idea, I felt like we needed to get IT and marketing working together more effectively again, as our agendas had deviated with IT focusing on new technology in more recent times. She did a great job increasing the transparency of what was happening in the IT organization, and our relationship led to the teams working even more effectively together.

It is also critical for the CMO to spend a lot of time with operators and people in the field to understand what they need and how they think. Being in the trenches and providing help when it is needed builds the credibility and knowledge that serves well when getting support for and implementing new things. Of course, building credibility by implementing tools and capabilities that make the businesses better is an important element in building the relationship as well. We got to a place where the people in the field felt they were part of my team, which was the ultimate compliment for not only what we did but how we did it.

Balancing Centralization and Decentralization

Nearly all organizations struggle with finding the right balance between what should be centralized and what should be decentralized. The reality is that it should be a hybrid and likely will evolve over time based on the circumstances of the company and the talent in the corporate center and in the field. There are several principles to be followed in finding the right balance. The business units must be held accountable for their financial results and feel like they have some control in their destiny in return for that accountability. The corporate entity must also feel like it is truly responsible for the results of each of the business units. More specialized functional expertise should be centralized, as it is challenging and inefficient to replicate it many times over. It is critical that much of the best and unique talent reside centrally in order to be a credible resource to the field. Finally, the personality traits of corporate resources are critical as well. These people need to be smart, have strong communication skills, find the right balance between being firm and flexible, and be patient and relatively egoless. Driving change from a corporate center when there is a strong operator mentality is hard and requires a thick skin. I often say you have to Weeble back up after being punched in the gut as people initially tell you your ideas don't have merit, but it can also be very satisfying as trust is earned and progress is made over time.

Ultimately it is important to determine who has decision rights when consensus isn't reached. Many companies waste a lot of time debating and negotiating, spending time fighting internal battles as opposed to external ones. One of the areas we struggled with in this regard was brand campaigns, particularly the Harrah's brand, which was the most numerous in terms of properties and the most disparate in the quality and depth of assets. No doubt it is challenging to develop a brand platform for properties that ranged from the resort beauty of Lake Tahoe to a riverboat with no hotel and minimal dining amenities and many variations in between. For nearly a decade we struggled in developing a positioning platform that was universally appreciated in large part because we were too inclusive in the creation process—and with brand everyone has an opinion in what is a very subjective arena. In 2010 working with BBDO San Francisco after Gary told us how much he disliked the existing campaign, we developed the brand campaign with the agency and a couple of people on my team and with much more modest input from the field (see Figure 5.1). In the end, the brand positioning was

FIGURE 5.1	Harrah's identity: "The Fun Place to Play"

THE FUN PLACE TO PLAY
Anchors the concept around the desire of our target customers to have a good time while having more ways to "win."

WELCOMING
Friendly. Providing customers with a gaming experience that is welcoming and not intimidating, where they feel they are among friends and other people like them.

Familiar. Customers walking into a Harrah's, whether to gamble, dine, socialize, or see a show, will feel comfortable and ready to enjoy the experiences that await.

OPTIMISTIC
Light-hearted. Harrah's doesn't take itself too seriously, and neither do the customers who love to play here—this comes to life through our service and our promotions.

American Spirit. Harrah's captures and embodies the entrepreneurial, "anything is possible" attitude that is a key component of American culture.

LIVELY
Celebratory. Harrah's will provide customers with an atmosphere that is fun to be in and where winning is celebrated across many levels and touchpoints.

Energetic. The feeling customers will get when they walk into a Harrah's as emphasized by the flashing lights, sounds, music, and the overall aesthetics of the casino.

the most well liked across the company by far of any previous Harrah's brand work. And even Gary liked it.

Creating Incentives and the Importance of Strategic Bonus Structures

I am a big believer in having bonus structures that incent the right behavior, and I am often surprised by how many companies rely solely on company performance-based programs. Too often companies expect certain behaviors they believe will drive results without putting financial meat around the specific activity, or they make the bonus such a small fraction of the compensation package that it is irrelevant. For those that directly drive revenue, there should be a meaningful variable component to compensation with a bonus with no cap. One client we are working with wants to increase the crossover between its retail and online business, especially after we quantified how much more valuable those customers that spent in both are. However, the company-wide incentive to spur cross-channel spend was only 1 percent of the bonus plan. As a result, there weren't many activities to drive this behavior, which was so valuable to the company, that were visible to customers or employees to move the needle. Managers at various levels did the mental math to determine the best return of their time for both themselves and the company and rightfully determined it wasn't on driving cross-channel behavior.

At Harrah's, we had eliminated the fiefdoms that are prevalent in the industry and generally operated with a view that the customers were the company's and did not belong to a particular market or brand. As a result, half of our revenue was derived from customers playing at a property other than their preferred one, whether that meant playing at a sister property close to where they lived or making a destination trip to Las Vegas, Lake Tahoe, or New Orleans.

However, in 2010 as part of the broad consumer research effort we did, we determined that there was still a $2 billion untapped opportunity for us to capture more of our Total Rewards members' play when they went to other markets. A great example is represented in the chart in Figure 5.2, which shows the dynamics of players in Chicagoland. If Chicago residents only played with us in Vegas, we only captured 22 percent of their share, as they were much more likely to stay at a competitor, basing their choice on room rate and quality of product to meet their needs. However, if they played at one of our two Chicago properties, we captured 48 percent of their share in Las Vegas, because they were getting strong offers from us based on their Chicago play and because perhaps they were higher tier so they would have a much better and more personalized service experience when in Las Vegas, which is very important to gamblers. This dynamic worked in the reverse as well: we saw more play in Chicago from customers who played at one of our Las Vegas properties.

To capture more of this opportunity, I proposed to senior management that we change the property bonus structure to include a cross-market component. Historically, the bonus was weighted 75 percent to how the property did achieving its EBITDA target, and 25 percent was based on customer service scores. We changed the model to 60 percent EBITDA, 20 percent service, and 20 percent cross-market play. To establish the cross-market component, we took the baseline of the revenue a property exported to other properties in the network (e.g., how much revenue from Philadelphia customers was captured in Atlantic City, Las Vegas, New Orleans, and Tahoe) and built the 20 percent target with stepwise hurdles to encourage growth in this number. It was amazing how many tactical activities started

FIGURE 5.2	Bidirectional value of x-market play

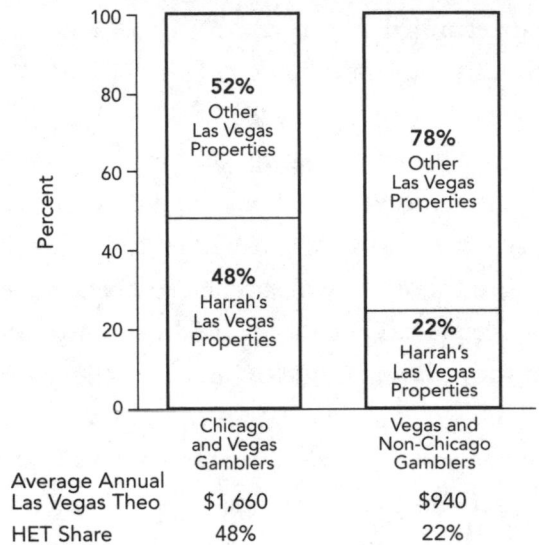

Chicago Residents Las Vegas Theo

Chicago and Vegas Gamblers
- 52% Other Las Vegas Properties
- 48% Harrah's Las Vegas Properties

Vegas and Non-Chicago Gamblers
- 78% Other Las Vegas Properties
- 22% Harrah's Las Vegas Properties

	Chicago and Vegas Gamblers	Vegas and Non-Chicago Gamblers
Average Annual Las Vegas Theo	$1,660	$940
HET Share	48%	22%

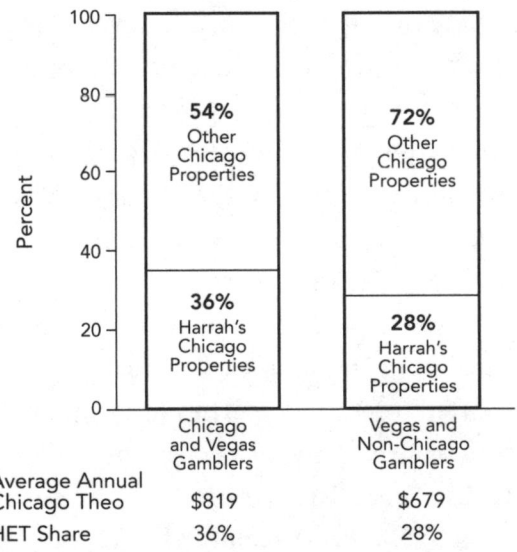

Chicago Residents Chicago Theo

Chicago and Vegas Gamblers
- 54% Other Chicago Properties
- 36% Harrah's Chicago Properties

Vegas and Non-Chicago Gamblers
- 72% Other Chicago Properties
- 28% Harrah's Chicago Properties

	Chicago and Vegas Gamblers	Vegas and Non-Chicago Gamblers
Average Annual Chicago Theo	$819	$679
HET Share	36%	28%

Source: Consumer Survey, August 2010; SSI full sample, Bain analysis.

taking place to highlight sister properties, including signage, videos, and promotions with trips to Vegas or Atlantic City. Total Rewards collateral became more prevalent, as that was the conduit and raison d'être to move people across the system.

A critical complement to the management bonus change was what we did to ensure that the hosts were even more motivated to send their customers to other properties for great events such as Celebrity Golf in Lake Tahoe or Jazz Fest in New Orleans. Previously, hosts would only get a bonus for cross-market play if they had achieved their revenue targets at their home property. Given that our VIP business was down dramatically after the economic crisis, this was a challenge in most if not all of our markets, so the hosts had little motivation to fill cross-property events. By relaxing this constraint, the hosts started filling these great events more willingly. We also did contests at the host level to increase awareness and awarded people with meaningful prizes such as iPads to increase the focus. We generated more than $20 million in incremental revenue in short order with these changes and further entangled our top customers by giving them amazing experiences in new markets that the local competitor could not match.

The key lesson is that while individual brand accountability is critical, ultimately the customer is the company's, and it is imperative to capture more share across all brands. We could prove analytically that as customers increased their number of property visits with us both within our multiproperty markets and across markets, their play level increased with us and a higher rate of revenue was retained year to year.

We have seen this reiterated with several clients across a range of industries. The chart in Figure 5.3 shows how much more profitable multibrand customers are and how few of the company's customers actually shopped all three brands. The trick is to model

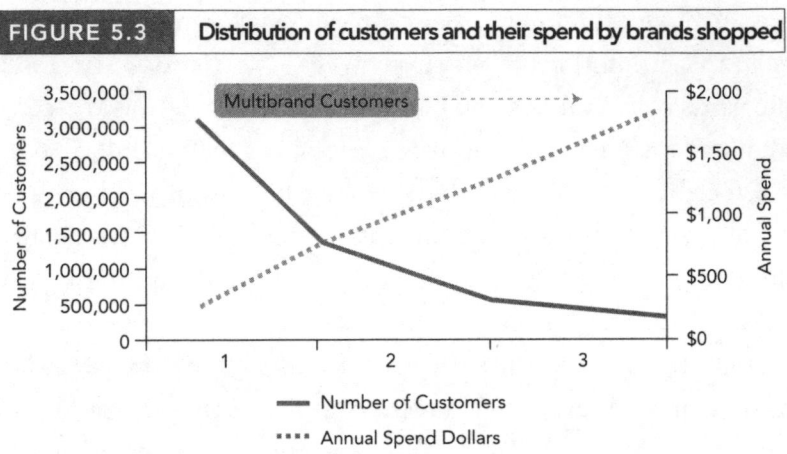

FIGURE 5.3   Distribution of customers and their spend by brands shopped

multibrand players and predict who of the low-value masses has the potential to shop across brands, which we were able to do based on a variety of demographic and behavioral factors. These folks can be targeted for very surgical marketing so as not to confuse the individual brand positioning in mass advertising.

Organizational dynamics are paramount to the success of driving transformational change. Having strong support from the top of the organization in combination with collaborative "bottom-up" processes leads to the best results. In addition, creating seamless working relationships across organizational lines leads to consensus and the best outcomes, though it seems it is a rare occurrence. Finally, it is an obvious statement, but incentive systems have to be aligned to drive the right behaviors. When all this comes together, true magic can happen for the company.

01110100 1110100110001011 111 0111
11 00 100011 110111101101010 101111

Doubling Down

- **Executive steering committees are essential to driving change.** They ensure that new ideas are fully baked and push adoption across the organization.

- **Diverse cross-functional task forces are critical.** They drive innovation, developing the ideas and plans for implementation to present to the executive steering committees.

- **CMO and CIO partnership is key.** Amazing things can happen when there is a strong bond between the CMO and CIO and when they take joint accountability for the vision and implementation of a project.

- **You can never spend too much time in the field.** For a corporate marketing leader, understanding operations and building relationships with operational leaders is the most valuable ingredient in creating relevant solutions.

- **Evolve the decentralized-centralized equilibrium point.** Constantly evolving the equilibrium point between centralized and decentralized leads to the best outcomes. Sadly, there is no universal truth to this age-old dilemma!

- **Incentive structures should have a blend of fixed and variable pay.** Multifaceted yet understandable incentive structures that reward a range of measurable objectives and have a strong mix of fixed and variable play lead to the best outcomes from motivated employees.

Hiring Practices

There are several consistent trends that I have seen that limit progress in making significant change toward customer centricity. The first is that the executives who do the hiring still have a very strong bias toward hiring people that have the specific industry experience the executives have. While, of course, there is merit to this in terms of the person's knowing what drives the business, more often than not it leads to modest incremental change as opposed to the transformational change that can occur when someone comes to the industry with a fresh perspective and the requisite other skills to have an impact.

Having led dramatic change in an organization is a unique skill and real-life experience that cannot be matched. I never hired a direct report from within the industry that wasn't internal to Harrah's, as I knew we were much more sophisticated than our competitors at the time from a marketing perspective. I hired people from top consulting firms and financial institutions who had demonstrated analytic and intellectual horsepower to help me innovate our marketing activities. There were a couple of more operational roles, such as the VP of VIP marketing position, where I would hire talented people from the field within Harrah's because of their operational credibility and knowledge, and that worked well. However, brand, digital, advertising, and other roles were all filled by non–casino people, as other industries simply were doing it better and I was most interested in their functional expertise.

The retail industry is particularly prone to hiring head marketers solely based on their having industry experience. Recently a leading brand that focuses on handbags was conducting a search, and the most important criterion given to the recruiters was that the candidates have luxury retail experience. The head internal recruiter told me, "They were not interested in someone with my background."

A study that Russell Reynolds Associates published in the summer of 2016 showed that of the 30 top retailers in the United States, 14 of them had replaced their CMO in the last 12 months. The authors of the study believe that the CMO role has evolved and fragmented in a way that retail marketers have to do more things than ever before, including having a deep understanding of digital, customer experience, technology, and analytics, and these skills haven't been developed well within the industry historically.

More specifically, Russell Reynolds identified eight reasons for the extremely high turnover among retail CMOs. They are presented in Figure 6.1.

Similarly, Heads International Executive Consultancy published an article in December 2016 articulating the need for financial services companies to be more progressive in their hiring of CMOs. The consultants urge their clients to be more disruptive in their hiring of the CMO and focus on those that

May 26, 2016

Richard Sanderson, Norm Yustin, Adam Twersky

| FIGURE 6.1 | Challenges for retail CMOs |

The ever-present Amazon threat and format shifts. There is increasing pressure to adapt business and marketing models to the Amazon juggernaut. eCommerce is both a sales and marketing channel, but is typically treated as a sales channel alone. CMOs who do not have full eCommerce responsibility are operating without control over one of their biggest marketing vehicles. While footsteps into retail locations have dropped significantly, brick and mortar sales have grown as the consumer is more informed, referencing twice as many sources before making a purchase. In some categories (for example, appliances) 90% of sales are web-influenced although 80% of sales still occur in a brick and mortar location.

Digital integration and mix complexity. While traditional retail traffic driving tactics are declining in effectiveness, many marketers are still trying to gain mastery of digital. Digital alone does not yet represent the silver bullet solution for most retailers. Today, media outlets are so fragmented that making a difference at scale has become more difficult than ever. Budgets and teams are spread too thinly among too many fragmented channels. Hence the mix has become more complex with more variables to optimize.

Loss of brand control. Most CMOs have increasingly less control over their brand. Consumers now have a louder voice, giving them a larger say in determining what a brand really is. Yesterday's CMO told the customer what their brand stood for. Today's CMO guides the brand by working internally to ensure the company meets the needs of the customer to build the brand.

Immediacy effect. If a CEO needs to buy time with his/her board, making a change in marketing leadership can offered as a signal of change.

Misalignment between operators and marketers. Retail GMs seek traffic driving and promotional activities to drive near-term operational results. Marketers typically have a longer-term view of metrics that drive returns. Both sides have a case. The marketer is the 'piggy in the middle' that balances the need to produce results with the need to be the voice of the customer and the devil's advocate that helps strengthen the overall business proposition. The balance can be hard to master.

The evolving skill set. CMOs, along with most business leaders, have historically been hired based on past experience. But what was successful 5 years ago may not work now. Experience is much less important versus agility and adaptability. Many marketers grew up in a world of advertising, positioning and branding. Now marketers are expected to master data, digital, customization and optimization. Rather than pivoting one way or the other, the key is to strike a balance of both. Instead learning agility and adaptation to new consumer shopper habits may matter more.

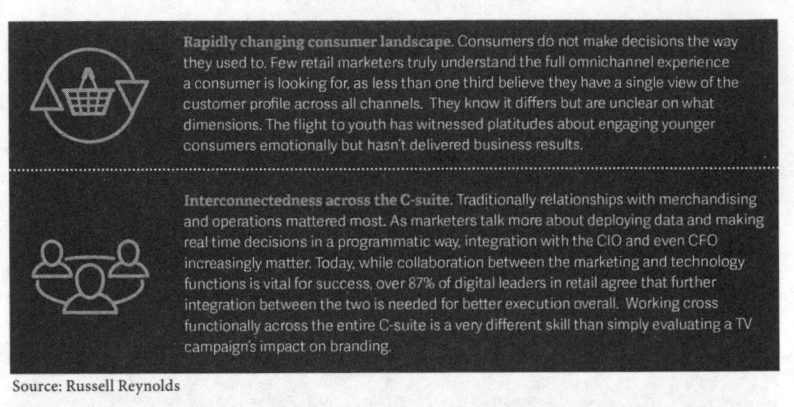

Rapidly changing consumer landscape. Consumers do not make decisions the way they used to. Few retail marketers truly understand the full omnichannel experience a consumer is looking for, as less than one third believe they have a single view of the customer profile across all channels. They know it differs but are unclear on what dimensions. The flight to youth has witnessed platitudes about engaging younger consumers emotionally but hasn't delivered business results.

Interconnectedness across the C-suite. Traditionally relationships with merchandising and operations mattered most. As marketers talk more about deploying data and making real time decisions in a programmatic way, integration with the CIO and even CFO increasingly matter. Today, while collaboration between the marketing and technology functions is vital for success, over 87% of digital leaders in retail agree that further integration between the two is needed for better execution overall. Working cross functionally across the entire C-suite is a very different skill than simply evaluating a TV campaign's impact on branding.

Source: Russell Reynolds

have "experience in defining and executing client-centric strategies" as opposed to only targeting those from within the industry. Heads International argues that the more complex landscape and increased customer demands call for a much more highly segmented approach and notes that banks have been slow to adapt to the wants and needs of their customers.

The other common bias in hiring is the fascination with CPG and brand experience. While I realize that brand building and advertising are very important, traditional advertising is very difficult to measure and is becoming slightly less important with the growth of new media channels and watching TV shows in a wide variety of ways becoming more prominent. In addition, the budgets for product and other launches are typically very large, with limited accountability for understanding incremental sales at a refined level. Often CPG and brand folks haven't had the experience with technology initiatives that are becoming such a critical component of the CMO's responsibilities as CMOs get more control of the IT budget. However, they still keep getting great jobs.

Making bad hiring decisions is one of the primary inhibitors to companies making progress in creating more customer- and data-driven organizations. Overrelying on industry and brand skills will bring about a modest evolution as opposed to seeking out those who have the appropriate skills to drive transformational change predicated on analytics and the ability to execute complex and technically driven initiatives.

```
01110100 11100100110001011 11100111
11 00 100011 110111101101010 101111
```

Doubling Down

- **Bad hiring practices impede change.** Maybe it goes without saying, but poor hiring practices limit a company's ability to implement successful transformational change. Good hiring practices speed innovation.

- **It's about more than industry experience.** Functional skills, analytic acumen, and demonstrated experience leading transformational change are just as critical as having industry experience—even more so when a company needs to evolve to survive and flourish.

Marketing Organizational Structure and Talent

One of the critical areas of discussion I have had with many CMOs is how to organize their team and how to determine what should be in marketing as opposed to other functions. My organization at Caesars evolved and grew over time based on the opportunity to support emerging channels, as we centralized more activities and garnered more credibility for being able to deliver value to operations. Broadly I was looking for analytically inquisitive people who were comfortable with numbers but also had good communication skills and the right amount of confidence, not crossing the line of arrogance where no one would want to work with them. While I tried to draw clear lines of responsibility between my direct reports' teams, there were shades of gray that required collaboration and seamless handoffs to be effective.

Broad Talent Themes

While the specifics are going to vary by circumstance, there are some broad themes that are transferable. It is imperative that marketing have its own analytical resources embedded within the organization as opposed to being reliant on analysts who are in Finance. The CMO needs go to resources, whose time and priorities are under the CMO's control, so that customer and program performance can be determined in a timely way and turned into action very quickly to drive needed results. Marketing analysts tend to have more of a revenue focus as opposed to those in finance, who are by nature cost control biased, and good analysts will pay for themselves many times over. The career path aspect of having analysts in marketing cannot be understated, as they want to be considered marketers now and as they progress in the future. They want to move up within marketing and gain knowledge of the various disciplines that are a critical part of being a great marketer. We developed close relationships with great centers of education like Wharton, Washington University, and Carnegie Mellon to have a strong source of new talent and a recurring hiring and onboarding process. One significant mistake that was made in a 2011 reorganization at Caesars was to move our world-class marketing analysis function into finance, which resulted in a significant amount of turnover and drain of talent from the company.

Marketing Analysis Managers

One of the best organizational moves we made occurred in 2004 when we created a group called the Marketing Analysis Managers, affectionately known as the MAMs. We had created standard reporting available at a click of a button that enabled field operators to understand business trends and marketing program performance in a very detailed way. However, the properties were not equipped with the resources to explore the deeper level and strategic questions about their business that would enable them to be even smarter and more surgical in their actions. To resolve this problem, we decided to hire MBA types. They would report to one of my most talented direct reports. Katrina Lane would be able to hire and train the best and brightest, something we wouldn't be able to replicate in each of our 30+ properties. She had spent seven years at McKinsey and fully understood how analytic consultants could add value.

The twist was that we would have them geographically dispersed so they would be able to understand a smaller number of markets in more detail and could spend a significant amount of time with the operators they supported. From a lifestyle perspective, the MAMs wouldn't have to travel from Las Vegas each week, as the properties they supported were relatively close. However, they benefited from the cross-pollination of knowledge through regular group calls where results were shared.

This group ended up being one of the best sources of new talent. The group members learned about the company's tools and strategies in a relatively safe environment since they were not responsible for the execution of revenue-driving activities on a daily basis, but they were also close enough to the operations to have credibility and knowledge. As a result, the operators raided this group regularly to fill critical property jobs, which was a terrific problem for my group though we had to continually hire new talent. When we expanded this group to do all the marketing analysis in 2010, it was the easiest proposition I ever sold to the operators, as the group had so much credibility as being true partners of the operators.

Dedicated Statisticians

Having a group of statisticians within marketing who can dive into the data and build models to improve marketing efficiency is critical as well. We had five statisticians who were dedicated to marketing and several more who were focused on hotel revenue management optimization, all of whom reported to a very smart and technically proficient vice president, Dave Kowal. The statisticians scored customers on a variety of levels and built highly segmented, automated queries and dozens of standard reports that enabled users to spend more time thinking about solutions as opposed to spending all their time running lists and reports.

The statisticians were not the most user-friendly and communicative talent on my team, so they were complemented by two more groups: one was an internal loyalty marketing consulting group, and the other was a marketing training team that provided the support and translation of new tools to the field both at the outset when launched and on an ongoing basis; these two groups reported to a separate vice president.

Creating Organizational Synergy

I found a lot of synergy by bucketing brand marketing, traditional, digital, and social media, email and mobile marketing, and an internal creative studio under one leader. Monica Sullivan is quite expert with digital and new media, and with two strong creative agencies and my involvement on the front end of new brand campaigns, we were able to have a very effective team. Having both an excellent grasp of the media and control of the purse strings enabled her to move money across channels based on the needs of the business and performance. Having the internal studio connected to the brand ensured that our brand campaigns came to life appropriately even in promotional as opposed to pure brand-building communication at a fraction of the cost of having the agencies do low-complexity work.

As described elsewhere in the book, we completely revolutionized the casino host function, adding science to a high-touch service experience. Brett Kline, the vice president who led the most significant change management projects we did, was responsible for the VIP host tools, which were built initially using Blue Martini and then migrated to Salesforce, and the VIP strategy and developing companywide VIP events. Even though there was a separate vice president of our loyalty program Total Rewards, responsibility for the upper-echelon tier resided in the VIP group to ensure that the benefits and services were unique and high touch. Brett did so well in this role because he had spent many years at properties in casino marketing and as an assistant general manager so he knew the operations well; he also had a great style about him that enabled him to solicit feedback and buy-in while being true to what needed to be done.

Another direct report was responsible for national promotions, events, alliances, and public relations. Many of our national promotions involved big national branded partners, and we leveraged PR significantly to create awareness to attract new customers. I also had a leader of multicultural marketing. The job of multicultural marketing was to ensure that we had not only in-language marketing communication but also relevant entertainment and the right amenities and cultural environment on property.

We started with domestic Asian customers and then added Hispanic marketing as more of a mass market approach to attract entertainment seekers. I also had Sandeep Khera focused on real-time interactive CRM, partnering closely with our IT and slots departments to develop, test, and execute a capability that enabled us to make relevant real-time offers to customers based on their historical profile, current trip activity, and available distressed assets. The VP of Total Rewards was responsible for evolving the value proposition of the program and ensuring that it was well integrated into newly acquired businesses.

Creating Culturally Relevant Interactions

Our decision to dedicate attention to building capabilities around domestic Asian customers was one of the best things that we did. I first proposed the notion of corporate market-ing, leading this effort at a Western Division planning meeting attended by at least 60 people. Like some other initiatives we had proposed, it was met with skepticism. People expressed doubt that corporate would be able to operationalize a strategy, and there wasn't much of a feeling that things needed to evolve beyond the current model of having a culturally relevant host and a noodle bar.

Four months later we came to the Operations Committee with a more fully baked plan informed by a significant research effort we had done. We talked to customers in key markets, including New York, Chicago, Houston, Los Angeles, and San Francisco, and interviewed Asian Americans of Chinese, Japanese, Korean, and Vietnamese descent. The most critical insights we learned were that many Asian American gamers were new in their accul-turation to the United States and that a meaningful portion of them were not fully comfortable speaking English. In addition, multiple generations lived together, which had several implications for our direct mail strategy.

We felt there was a significant upside to creating more culturally relevant and sensitive interactions across all their experiences on property, and there was an opportunity to grow what was already a several hundred million dollar business by creating the best experience for our customers of Asian descent. In our proposal to the Operations Committee we asked for $4 million to build out an organization and capabilities to capture this opportunity, and we received vigorous support.

We hired a leader, Richard Fu, who had previously worked at a major financial services institution heading a multicultural marketing team, and a strong number two person as a starting point, and we engaged a respected New York City–based Asian agency that had worked with great brands in their domestic Asian efforts. We were also fortunate to have two great partners in Saul Gitlin and Cynthia Park from the agency, who helped us accelerate our efforts and develop the path forward.

We created in-language advertising materials, including TV spots and print, in the appropriate Asian publications. We developed on-property signage and collateral in the various languages to help these customers feel more comfortable on property, and we educated them on Total Rewards as we knew there would be more hesitancy about having play tracked than there was with the general population.

Another critical initiative was doing cultural awareness and sensitivity training for frontline employees. This helped them understand the nuances that would enable them to deliver a higher level of personalized service.

Finally, we built beautiful Asian-themed gaming and dining areas in a dozen of our properties. The areas were designed by a great partner, Taki Murao, and provided amazing environments for our customers to play and eat in. These collective efforts enabled us to grow this business by 25+ percent, representing more than $600 million of our revenue.

Sustaining Quality Training and Fostering Positive Change

One of the unique and important things we did in 2003 was to create a marketing training team within my group. We found that we did not have a good process to onboard new marketers in the field, and as a result many new hires from outside the company who started as property marketers did not succeed.

Because the subject matter was intensely marketing and technically focused, we chose to provide this training in the marketing department as opposed to human resources. We developed a several-day "Marketing the Harrah's Way" class, which helped close the gap between what was being executed in our distributed field operations and what was possible; we covered a spectrum of subjects because we had people from various levels, ranging from general manager to financial analyst, attend the class. Many of my direct reports presented during the week, as did critical partners in functions such as finance and information technology; this helped build critical bonds early in the tenure of the new employees. As time went by, many marketers had heard about the Harrah's marketing story, and that had attracted them to the role even if it was in the field. This onboarding class helped codify the new employees' decision to join and more importantly helped them hit the ground running.

It is also very important to infuse new talent into the team periodically to continue to progress. Clearly it is a manger's role to guide and nurture people and the team, enabling them to grow and progress beyond what they thought was possible. However, there are times when changes need to be made if people have approached the limit of their capabilities. Twice in my 12-year tenure at Harrah's, I fairly dramatically turned over my direct report team. The first time was in 2003, four years into our journey during which we achieved great success. However, most of the original direct reports had come up through the operations, which was important both to help me understand the practicalities of implementation since I was new to the industry and to build credibility with the field. The downside was that these people were not very strategic and couldn't push the thinking of new ideas; they were excellent at implementing well-baked ideas.

After going through the proper HR processes and finding soft landing spots in the field for most of them, I brought in a new wave of talent, like Katrina Lane and Marc Oppenheimer, who had terrific academic and professional pedigrees including Stanford, Northwestern, Harvard, McKinsey, and Bain. This talent helped challenge my thinking and gave me needed scale, given the additional responsibilities I had taken on. As all good managers know, one's own success is dependent on having good people as your partners, and that is even more critical as you achieve executive status in your organization. Trying to take on too much on their own is a very common mistake that I see people make. There is a limit to everyone's bandwidth and range of knowledge; having great people around you is best for you and your company.

I replaced four direct reports at the end of 2009 as well, as I needed transformational change after the economic downturn severely impacted the casino industry. In each instance, I worked closely with the individuals to articulate the need for change, and I provided a road map for how it could be done along with action plans and timelines.

For example, the retail stores for Caesars had been very successful for a long period, driving significant profit and healthy margins. However, with a glut of high-end shopping throughout Las Vegas, I knew we needed to create more exceptional and experiential retail to drive traffic to our properties. Unfortunately, the leader of that function wasn't willing or able to operate the business differently.

Our branch office sales network was another example. Historically it had done a very good job servicing existing customers and helping drive high-revenue retention rates. But after the gaming budget of VIPs was hit hard, we needed that group to be much more sales focused, which required significant training of the current team and more likely turnover. The direct reports for these areas and a couple of others either didn't buy into the new vision or didn't have the ability to push the agenda forward. This inevitably resulted in the changes and the infusion of new talent to help execute in the new world.

It is never easy to let go of good people who have been an integral part of your and the company's success. Still, in each of the circumstances in 2003 and 2009 I knew it was the right thing to do based on what was needed for the company as a whole, and the expectations had been stated clearly. As long as people are given the chance to develop and help define and execute a new vision, and are treated with dignity and humanity on the back end, you have done all you can as a manager.

Personal resilience is also a very important trait for CMOs to exhibit. When the company is behind plan, the head marketer is typically the first target the CEO focuses on. There are going to be ups and downs whether fair or not, and you must self-reflect and identify what you can do to turn things around and change the status quo. It does no good to sulk or quit, and it is a good opportunity to work smarter and harder and prove people wrong.

Organizational design is a critical element of the CMO's job, and much thought and consideration should be given to it. Finding the balance between the optimal structure and the ability and skills of the team is essential to create clear areas of autonomy and to manage the shades of gray that can exist across functions. To sustain this balance, the successful organization must be committed to regularly evolving and optimizing the structure to nurture talent and increase synergy.

```
01110100 111001001100001011 11100111
11 00 100011 110111101101101010 101111
```

Doubling Down

- **You need analytic resource in your direct control.** As a marketer, this lets you make informed decisions as quickly as possible without waiting in a queue.

- **Statisticians and data scientists are essential to creating insights.** The output of their work will help drive a refined level of personalization that will delight your customers.

- **Cultural awareness and sensitivity matters.** This attentiveness will be recognized and appreciated by your customers and lead to deeper levels of loyalty.

- **Ongoing training processes are essential.** Many companies effectively train employees during the rollout of new capabilities; very few have an ongoing process to onboard new employees to ensure they can be successful as quickly as possible.

- **It is imperative that you have great people on your team to give you scale.** This is vital even if that means driving change among your direct reports!

Using External Resources

While my bias was always to hire smart people and drive innovation internally, there were certainly times when integrating external experts and provocateurs into the team was critical to our success. As one example, early on we brought in a third party to help complete the more complicated system integration work needed for the launch of our original website at Harrah's. In working with them to finish that project, we learned that they had a very strong process related to marketing-driven technology projects that enabled us to explore a range of solutions before breaking the project into reasonable chunks of deliverables. We worked with them several times in future projects, adopted its process for our technology projects, and hired a couple of talented people from there to join our IT group at Harrah's.

As another early example, we realized we needed external experts when we decided to pursue domestic Asian customers in a more culturally sensitive and personalized way. While we had managed the business fairly effectively previously, we knew if we were going to engage this customer base in a more relevant way, we should hire a resource that had engaged with Asian Americans for other strong brands. We investigated several agencies and selected Kang & Lee, based on its strong portfolio of clients, to help us optimize the opportunity. This New York City agency helped us develop the strategy and execute the game plan that facilitated our ability to build deeper relationships with these customers.

We didn't often use the well-known strategy consultants, but we had several successful initiatives with Bain, Booz, and McKinsey, as our approach was to be extremely integrated at various levels with their project teams, with deep involvement from me, a direct report or two who were nearly dedicated to the effort, and various manager-level people who were highly involved as well. Given the level of sophistication of our marketing activities, the consultants needed to step up their game from their typical client engagements in order to add value. The answers were not as simple as a percent reduction here and there.

It is critical to embrace external consultants as additional resources that can help get more done because of both their intellectual horsepower and the senior management visibility they often have. While it can be frustrating that they get credit for ideas from you and your team, it is best to embrace the opportunity to drive change; get on board or be seen as an obstacle to progress, which is not a good place to be.

Planning for Success

We had good success with McKinsey on a significant teleservices project that redefined how we handled our inbound reservations calls in a dramatic and controversial way to the operators, as we were migrating from small call centers in each property that the operators controlled to two large ones in Atlantic City and Las Vegas. This was a significant change management initiative that the operators strongly opposed, as they felt that local knowledge was critical to having a successful call that would lead to a hotel booking. The project ended up being a big success because I had my top direct report spend a significant portion of her time driving it and we developed a plan that elevated our service levels while simultaneously drastically reducing our costs.

Booz helped us with a project that enabled us to reduce 10 percent ($50 million) of our marketing service expenses without threatening the customer experience, primarily by consolidating the number of vendors that the properties were using to buy promotional services or execute direct mail. One of our best projects was a strategic segmentation effort with Bain Consulting that resulted in several unexpected changes; these included altering the management bonus to incorporate a component based on cross-business revenue and refining our media planning decisions based on where the revenue opportunity was building upon our new strategic segmentation scheme.

There were also several challenging projects with consultants, given how sophisticated we were in our marketing activity. On a couple of occasions, a brash junior consultant or engagement manager would think she or he had all the answers, based on her or his modest experience, or would force a project approach with the tried and true method of reducing marketing cost by x percent when the answer was significantly more complex and nuanced than that. This was the case with a project we did in the fourth quarter of 2008 in an effort to reduce marketing expense with our drastically lower revenues after the economic crisis. While the percent reduction method worked fairly well on a parallel labor efficiency effort, it would have led to suboptimal if not disastrous results on the marketing front. We had much debate with the consulting firm in team meetings and in front of the executive team to make sure we didn't bite off our nose to spite our face to further impact revenue with across-the-board marketing expense reductions. Some key people on my team, such as Dave Kowal and Bob Brown, really stepped up to develop compelling direct marketing innovations that made our marketing even more sophisticated and effective than it had been before. So while the direct output of the consulting firm was not used, the process led us to push ourselves further than we otherwise might have.

Managing Difficult Consulting Relationships

There was another frustrating mandated consulting-led effort a couple of years prior that was focused on reducing corporate and divisional expense that we labeled "CDR." In the first several years of my tenure at Harrah's, we had three regionally based divisions, with Gary Loveman serving as the COO. When he got promoted to CEO at the end of 2002, one of those three regional presidents was promoted to COO; the other two were given larger regions to run as a consolation prize. However, both were disappointed they were not chosen to be COO, and in a form of protest, each hired significant regional teams that created in essence shadow corporate organizations—and this led to a proliferation of cost, not to mention increased organizational tension. Soon after that time, Harrah's acquired Caesars, nearly doubling the size of the company from a revenue perspective. The thesis of the Caesars deal was much more about revenue synergy and growth than about cost savings, and significant corporate infrastructure was added in the name of elevating the Harrah's culture from the

Walmart of gaming to a more luxury-oriented one with our new Caesars brand asset.

There was good reason to do this CDR project, because the combined corporate and regional cost had increased dramatically as a percentage of revenue even with our revenue having doubled. In addition, we were preparing for a private equity transaction, as we learned in retrospect, so there was a strong desire to improve profitability to secure the most lucrative deal possible. However, the consultants came in with their tried and true approach of focusing on reducing corporate expense as a percentage of revenue as the primary objective function as opposed to diving deeper to truly understand the dynamics of what was working and where the opportunities were to reduce waste. As recommendations came forth during the project, there were many heated discussions in which I argued for doing what was best and not being totally focused on one objective function of reducing corporate expense. One particularly annoying example occurred when one of the division presidents pushed to reduce the two Marketing Analysis Manager positions supporting his division, even though as mentioned earlier, the MAM group had been critical to improving our marketing effectiveness. He argued that he had analysis covered in his division, and the executive team allowed that perspective to win.

Another poorly constructed consulting project in 2010 was focused on how to salvage the Atlantic City, New Jersey, market, which was in a deep downward spiral with the spread of gaming in Pennsylvania and New York. We had nearly half of the market revenue with four properties in Atlantic City (Bally's, Caesars, Harrah's, and Showboat). The decision was made to partner with a large, traditional consulting firm that we had worked with on several projects over the years. However, from the outset it was clear that this effort was not in the firm's wheelhouse, and we had to change the engagement manager and client lead within the first couple of weeks, as they were combative and ineffective for what was needed.

I visited Atlantic City nearly every month during my time at Harrah's and saw it evolve from a market monopoly cash cow to one that was besieged by regional competition that had reduced market revenue in half (see Figure 8.1).

The reality was that the vast majority of the customer base now had gaming options in their backyard and there was no longer the need to drive 60+ miles each way, particularly in the winter months, in order to fill their gaming fix. There had been attempts to add nongaming revenue, motivated most notably by the initial and continued success of the Borgata, which has an array of high-end amenities. But the nongaming revenue continued to be a fraction of gaming revenue in Atlantic City. There were several fundamental reasons for this relative to the success of Las Vegas where more than half of the revenue is nongaming, including the reputation and marketing of the city, the number of hotel rooms available, the weather other than the summer months, and the quality of the casino resorts.

| FIGURE 8.1 | AC market as a case study |

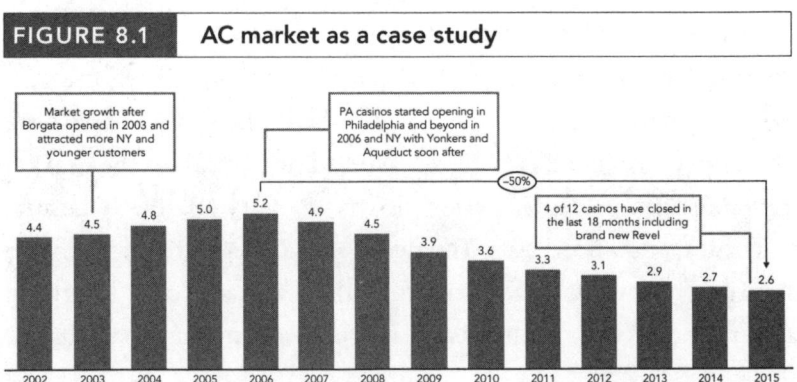

We knew revitalizing Atlantic City was a hard problem that would require creative thinking with those who had experience with urban redevelopment, so we sought out a different resource from the standard management consulting firm. We decided to partner with a company that had worked on projects such as the High Line in New York City, the Navy Yard area in Washington, D.C., and downtown Cincinnati.

Together with the urban planning firm, we looked at South Beach as a relevant example of an area that had transformed in an interesting way with its hotels, nightlife, and arts scenes. We felt like we needed to attract a different resident to Atlantic City through ventures like a culinary school or through art studios to create a larger and more compelling population base. We knew that the dilapidated buildings had to come down to create open space and a more positive perception of the city and that more than $8 million a year had to be spent by the Visitors Authority to promote and change the perception of the market in the key feeder markets of Philadelphia and New York City. Collectively as a market we did some new and interesting things, like holding concerts on the beach, a Tribeca film festival on the beach, and a Wine and Food Festival. Our goal was to attract a new consumer, someone other than the 70+ year-old slot player who was not coming nearly as often since the same slot product was available in Philadelphia and New York.

While the output of this effort was incorporated in Governor Christie's Atlantic City rescue plan, ultimately billions of dollars of capital were required to truly change the market as an entertainment destination and to create an attractive residential area. Unfortunately, unlike Cincinnati that had Procter & Gamble as its anchor local invested corporation, or D.C. that had Nationals Park, or San Francisco that had AT&T Park as hubs to build around, Atlantic City had a lack of corporations in the area; there were not enough companies that had a reason to step up to invest and implement the plan. As a result, Atlantic City continues to decline, and New Jersey has considered allowing gaming in the northern part of the state to increase its tax base and siphon off revenue from Pennsylvania and New York casinos.

There are several lessons to be learned from these various projects with consultants. The first is to recognize that the consultant firm has been brought in by the CEO for a reason, right or wrong. It is best to embrace the situation and leverage it to promote positive change, as large consulting firms have the ear of the CEO and the executive team. It is important to find the balance between being open to new ideas and areas for improvement and pushing to maintain some elements of the status quo that are working well. It is critical to spend time educating the consulting firm on the front end of the project, and it is worth dedicating a strong resource or two from your organization to the core team to help drive the agenda and increase the knowledge base of the collective team. The best projects we did with consultants are when the teams were integrated and cohesive as opposed to having an us-versus-them mentality.

Optimal Models

We engaged with agencies by taking the approach of having more partners with specific expertise as the optimal model as opposed to trying to consolidate within one broader full-service firm. If an agency holding company can seamlessly bring together multiple agencies, that can be a very successful model too, though I think it does require both a senior agency resource to truly understand the business and a generalist project manager to coordinate and organize activities. We had two creative agencies that focused on specific brands (GSD&M for Caesars and Horseshoe and BBDO West for Harrah's, World Series of Poker, Total Rewards, and the ancillary brands). We had a media planning agency as well as a digital one that placed and evaluated all our online advertising. In each instance, my team members were very hands-on with the day-to-day execution and long-range planning in a very integrated way.

We did rely on a number of technical providers to help implement our capabilities, ranging from Teradata, SAS, Unica, TIBCO, Salesforce, and many others. Generally, we found that they added a lot of value in enhancing the technical aspects of our infrastructure but not as much in identifying the business and strategic opportunities. While we typically did a lot of customization when implementing technology, one of our key lessons learned was that you could go too far with customization, as it had implications for the implementation timeline. Also, too much customization hindered our ability to take advantage of enhancements that vendors make to their product on a frequent basis, the problem being that the more customization there was, the more backward integration was required when new versions came out.

There are challenges and gaps with external resources when it comes to implementing a CRM approach. Management consultants provide strategic direction that can be helpful but not the specific actions and the tools to execute the plans. Conversely, technology firms provide a mechanism to execute but don't provide a road map and often the insight on what to execute in order to fully leverage their tool. While Salesforce, Merkle, and others have attempted to add a consulting layer to their robust platforms, it seems that their success has been modest. While it could be a profitable recurring revenue stream for them, their combined focus and orientation is still geared to product sales and ongoing licensing fees. In both situations, the firm has made a significant investment, potentially without immediate tangible value, which creates pressure that can spiral throughout the organization.

This is what we are solving for now at GALE: providing deep analytic-based strategic insight and an ability to take action quickly to drive business results that build momentum for a more customer-centric and analytic approach. Combining strategy, technology, and execution seamlessly and quickly has been a significant part of our value proposition.

Adapting to the Growth of Digital

There is significant change taking place in the marketing services world, and agencies are struggling to adapt. There is always going to be a place for brilliant creative and TV advertising, and there are many firms that are doing that exceptionally well. While a new brand platform can be a critical tool in a company's strategic repositioning, I believe it is the rare occurrence that a brand agency is an important strategic thought partner for the CMO, much less the CEO. There generally isn't enough context about the overall business and operational performance to be a trusted advisor about what to do beyond mass communication.

Agencies have adapted to the growth of digital and have added capabilities in that area, but generally it is more about taking their television campaigns and making them videos on the site. Most have not built solutions for their clients that account for digital in the broadest sense of the term. And there is still a lack of measurability on traditional media spend, for which clients have not demanded more rigor to understand the return on investment. That and the desire to see spots more often on TV, have a Super Bowl ad that creates buzz, or winning awards will lead to a focus on commercials by top agencies.

Many clients are seeking integrated agency solutions, looking for the benefit of having deep functional expertise from several disciplines and/or geographies without the hassle of having to deal with multiple agencies from a logistics point of view as it relates to meetings and processing payments. I have seen this in several formal pitch processes where potential clients test out the camaraderie of the various agency teams and request case studies showing how the agencies worked together in the past. Agencies, even if they are sister ones, are willing to participate that way to get a foot in the door in the hopes they can capture more of the business once they are in. There are still other challenges with this approach, whether it be the back-end process coordination to make it seamless for the client to pay bills or the competitive juices that cause a firm to increase its own revenue as opposed to thinking about the greater good and what is best for the client.

I think there are a couple of critical reasons why this integrated agency approach has not taken a greater hold other than the rare extremely large client relationships that warrant a dedicated cross-discipline team despite many holding companies building attempted solutions for this. The first is that the organizational structure on the client side in some instances doesn't allow for an integrated approach across channels or business units. This occurs when there are marketing leaders by region or business unit or senior functional leaders by marketing discipline who want to have their own agency that they can direct. The second critical reason is that budgets may be in organizational silos, and there may not be an arbitration process to resolve how best to prioritize marketing resources other than a time-consuming annual process.

I have also experienced recently two large pitches where the client and search consultant were explicitly looking for an integrated approach across agencies with different areas of expertise. The first instinct of the holding companies is to still lead with a brand agency and creative messaging–led platform paying little attention to what is in the brief—and more telling, not listening to the client and consultant carefully along the way about what the business really needs.

In both instances, the lead story in the pitch was a brand positioning platform with lots of fancy creative-led TV ads that were well done. However, the prospective clients in both situations were looking for a deeper understanding of their target customers and a demonstrated ability to interact with them in a highly personalized way through digital channels, whenever and wherever their customers were in their journey with the brand. In the end, the clients chose digitally focused agencies as opposed to creative-led ones. We had the digital expertise in the room on our side, but that was made secondary as part of the pitch process.

Effectively leveraging external resources is critical to a CMO's success. It is imperative that an integrated and cohesive partnership is created and the external firm is not viewed as a vendor. The marketing services world is evolving rapidly, and some agencies are not adapting quickly enough. It is important to choose the right lead agency—one that is most comfortable in using analytics and digital technology. The combination of finding the right set of partners and having them work collaboratively creates the best chance of successful outcomes.

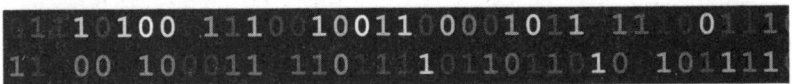

Doubling Down

- **Don't be afraid to seek out external experts.** They can help you push the agenda forward. (Even if they're forced upon you by the CEO or CFO, you should embrace them!)

- **Take an integrated approach.** It's equally important that these outside experts are up to speed as it is that your team can learn from them.

- **Don't rely on providers to drive the best utilization of their tools.** Technology and software providers have not fully developed solutions that allow clients to most effectively use their tools, and traditional consulting firms struggle executing the ideas they present to senior management.

- **Balance functional expertise with a holistic approach.** The agency landscape is changing quickly; ensure you get deep functional expertise.

Sales and "VIP" Service Providers

The most underrated thing we did at Harrah's—at least to external eyes, based on what has been publicized—was revolutionizing the casino host business. Hosts are analogous to personal shoppers or financial planners that manage the experience for the top customers. In the first few years I was at Harrah's, the focus of all our capability development was below the VIP level, partly because there was a belief within the company that outsiders to the industry shouldn't touch the VIP business. And from 1999 to 2002 we grew revenue from customers below the VIP level 15 to 20 percent each year because of all the things we had implemented that impacted that audience, while VIP revenue was flat. At the end of 2002, we made a pitch to develop capabilities at the VIP level in Corporate Marketing; we wanted to add some science to the high-touch personal service that was critical to the high-end customer experience. While there was a large dose of skepticism from the operators, we were given the green light to pursue this when the corporate leader of the VIP function left the company.

The initial insight was that our hosts were spending all their time with the very loyal guests who came quite frequently, much like we had spent all our marketing dollars courting those customers who were already coming all the time before we launched our life cycle direct marketing segmentation approach in 1999. While keeping those customers happy and retaining their revenue was critical, we wanted the hosts to nurture relationships with new, nonloyal, and defecting customers to grow the business.

We told the hosts that one day a week they would be back of house (not on the casino floor) calling customers in those opportunity segments to persuade them to have our casino be the customers' preferred one, stealing trips and market share from competitors. This required the hosts to have sales skills in addition to service ones, so we conducted training sessions to teach selling techniques. The initial reaction from these powerful and long-tenured hosts was quite negative, but eventually they embraced it as they came to understand how the new compensation scheme worked, with a variable bonus only being paid when they grew their portfolio. During the initial training, we could tell that 20 to 25 percent of the hosts would struggle to make it in the new world because of a lack of sales acumen. We conducted remedial training to help them get there but did realize eventually that some would have to move on.

Another critical insight was that much of the knowledge about the customer was in the host's little black book or in the host's head. In addition, hosts did not have much insight into the customer's patterns of behavior in markets other than their own, and many of our best customers did visit multiple properties. Furthermore, the host manager didn't have any insight into what the hosts were doing both with their activities and with the outcomes, as customers were inconsistently coded to an individual host level.

We developed a "clienteling" solution using Blue Martini that provided a variety of benefits. The new system gave the hosts ready access to a wide range of information about their customers, including all their play history, current offers and point balance, and a variety of their service preferences. The hosts could also book rooms using a web-based application that mirrored our consumer-facing web solution. The leads were provided to them through the system based on their manager's prioritization, which was another key benefit of the system. The manager could have hosts focus on calling new customers to secure a second trip one day and the next day ask the hosts to work a list to help fill a blackjack tournament. The manager had much more transparency into the activities of the hosts and the outcome of their efforts, as the manager could easily see how each host's portfolio performed after we cleaned up the coding.

Our work in the VIP area was the first of several instances where we complemented a strategy and technical capabilities in what I referred to as an HR toolkit. This consisted of doing an assessment of the current talent, training the existing people, and identifying employees that would struggle to meet the requirements of the refined role. Other tools included a new performance appraisal form, a revised bonus program, structured interview questions for new hires, and a development program to help grow talent. Developing the HR processes was critical to enabling our projects to be a success. These processes helped ensure that all 900 hosts were receiving the coaching and feedback they needed to be successful and provided tangible metrics that could be easily communicated by their manager in short monthly reviews as well as the former annual process.

The work we did in the VIP area is very applicable to personal shopping in retail and to financial planners in financial services. In most retail environments, a personal shopper is reserved for only the very top customers, and the dynamics are similar to the ones we saw earlier, with the individual employees holding the knowledge either in their head or in their version of the little black book. The company is at risk if the employees leave, and the customers suffer if they visit the store and their host is not there or if they go to another market while traveling. Having the knowledge available in a customer contact system accessible via a mobile device for employees can greatly enhance the customer experience, as having a history of what the customers purchased in the past and what they are exploring online will greatly personalize the customer experience and help the employee suggest what items are best for the customers to consider next. In our research on the behalf of several retail clients, we have found that shoppers may not be comfortable deciding what items go together or determining if an item fits their style. Having someone who has insight about them is very reassuring in the shopping process. I believe customers are going to increasingly appreciate and demand this type of technology and service delivery from retailers.

Automation allows scaling of VIP service to more customers and facilitates a more seamless experience as customers interact with the brand across geographies. Finding the right balance of technology and human touch with your best customers is a great way to lock in their loyalty.

`01110100 11100100110001011 11100111`
`11 00 100011 11011110110110110 101111`

Doubling Down

- **Don't only focus on the most loyal customers.** High-touch employees who take care of your best customers also need to spend some of their time nurturing nonloyal customers who have high potential in order to drive incremental revenue.

- **Technology is key.** This allows the high-touch experience to scale to more customers, providing a more seamless experience across the brand, and it also protects the company from having important customer knowledge leaving with an employee.

- **Incentives go hand in hand with the strategy.** Make sure to build in a robust incentive program that is in close alignment with your business strategy in order to maximize results.

Customer Service and Contact Centers

When people think about omnichannel solutions, call centers aren't the first thing that comes to mind, as they are often viewed as operational cost centers. However, service channels can and should be critical opportunities to build relationships with customers via personalized interactions that leverage insight about who they are and their interactions with the brand. Providing a relevant and seamless experience across service channels leads to a much happier customer. Having had responsibility for call center operations at MBNA, American Express, and Harrah's, I have always thought of the contact center as a crucial marketing channel in addition to being a means to secure brand loyalty by exceeding service expectations.

FIGURE 10.1	Omnichannel experience

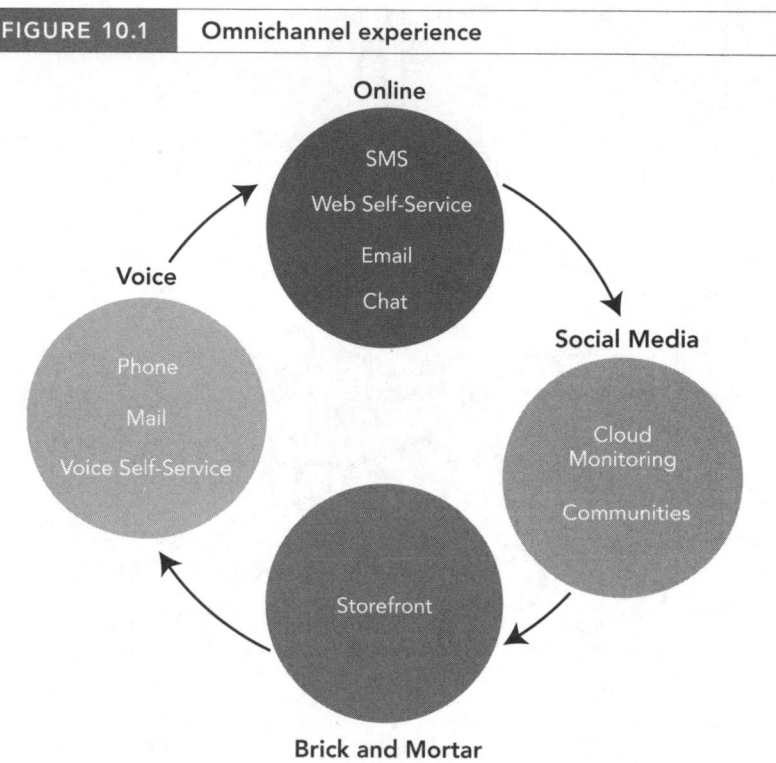

Customers increasingly want a seamless experience across touchpoints with a brand (Figure 10.1), and contact channels are often one of the greatest frustration points when the unfortunate call center rep does not have immediate access to all the customer history.

There has been an aggressive movement by many companies to take more calls offshore, with India initially being the primary location and then the Philippines becoming a significant hub of call center activity. There are nearshore options in Jamaica and throughout Central America as well. While the cost is often half as much when taking calls outside the United States, the impact on lifetime value of lower-quality service is often not measured quantitatively to determine if offshoring is the right answer. At the very least, the decision should be made in a refined way based on the value of customer satisfaction to understand where the tipping point is at various levels of customer profit. That is, for which level of customer should calls be taken in the United States to ensure a higher service standard?

Developing a Successful CEA Strategy

In October 2014, I took over an $80 million call center operation that MDC owned called Accent. The operation faced the significant challenges of having a small domestic footprint and heavy concentration with one client that was moving its volume rapidly to the Philippines in order to eliminate hundreds of millions of dollars of operating costs. Our price point at Accent was high, nearly twice as much as the client's cost from offshore providers, and our services levels were not exemplary, as the client detailed in a report done before I arrived. The client company made it very clear what Accent needed to do in order to stay on the provider list as the company dramatically reduced calls and the number of call center vendors.

To ensure Accent's survival in the absence of capital infusion and an ability to develop an offshore presence as dictated by MDC, we had to reposition Accent from a call center business process outsourcer (BPO) to a customer engagement agency (CEA). There were several critical elements of our mission to pivot Accent to a CEA, some of which we had the credibility to deliver and others we would have to rapidly develop to prove the model (Figure 10.2).

The first critical element was the ability to use data to have continuity across service channels, including inbound phone calls, e-care, chat, and social channel service. This entailed having a

FIGURE 10.2   Customer engagement agency defined

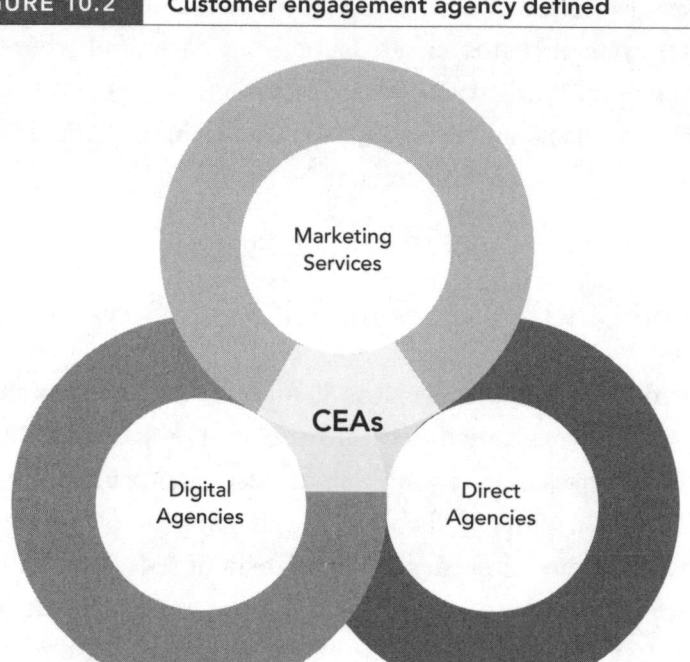

CRM database that kept track of interactions and could be accessed for the next customer interaction seamlessly. We had a couple of strong analysts within Accent that we partnered with a couple of talented analysts on my MDC team. Their job was to prove out the model quickly without adding cost while we determined if and how much clients would pay for different analytic insights than the standard phone metrics that call centers typically provide.

Another key element of our CEA strategy was the ability to have relevant conversations with the CMOs of our clients. Often the marketing department doesn't have an interest or say in call center operations, but the reality is that the call center is a critical place to convert demand stimulated by marketing activities into revenue. In addition, critical data can be captured in these service interactions that can be used to personalize content even further in marketing communications. Because of both the focus we had developed at Accent and my experience as a CMO, we were able to have regular and meaningful conversations with the CMOs of our clients and help them achieve their goals by better understanding their customers and creating ways for them to leverage the service channels to build brand equity and revenue.

Identifying Pain Points to Improve the Customer Experience

As we initiated our work with clients, we thought about the entire customer experience to identify pain points that led to leakage of revenue and negative customer sentiment. One example of this was with a large retailer that has more than 2,000 stores in the United States. This company's service model on the surface was very customer focused, as its internal name for the customer was highly complementary. However, calls were directed to each store, and there was little insight into the key metrics, such as abandon rate, speed of answer, and conversion. As part of our onboarding process, we did an audit of 20 stores to better understand what was happening from a customer perspective in the store. What we found is that many calls were going unanswered or people were put on hold as associates focused on customers that were there in the store. When associates did talk to customers on the phone, they more times than not told the customers just to show up when they wanted to come in as opposed to setting a firm time, which would have helped to ensure that the when the customers arrived there wouldn't be an overabundance of people arriving at the same time, creating a poor experience given a store's fixed capacity at any given moment.

Of course, our objective as a call center operator was to have more calls come to us so we could monetize the relationship with the client, but we knew there would be resistance from the store operations, which had historically had the power within the client organization. We suggested that we do a pilot of taking overflow calls from 50 stores to prove what incremental revenue could be captured and how significantly the service experience could be improved. The pilot got off to a fast start, and the head of stores pushed for an aggressive rollout; he and the CMO now had visibility to the baseline service metrics and the potential to manage customers in a better way, and the implications on revenue.

In addition to improving the customers' phone experience, we realized that many customers would want to make appointments in digital channels as opposed to having to call into a store with fixed operating hours. As a result, we explored online appointment systems, identified the best-in-breed product, and helped drive the implementation of it and the business rules to ensure operational acceptance. A subsequent phase integrated the appointment solution with the inventory system to ensure that the right product was available for the customers when they arrived, and this phase also facilitated cross-selling and upselling on the phone.

We also developed chat and social service for this client and others, realizing that customers want to interact with brands in real time through their mobile devices. Chat is a very effective way to walk customers through operational solutions and web interactions, and it scales effectively since agents can handle several conversations simultaneously.

Many agencies have created solutions to measure top-of-the-funnel social metrics such as likes, followers, etc., but we felt it was important to deliver customer-specific service solutions in the social channel as well. One of the critical reasons to deliver this service is that consumers can spread negative sentiment very quickly in social channels, and we wanted to be able to diffuse negativity and turn people into advocates by solving their issue quickly and efficiently through social.

We created a vision of the future state for this client that they could use to rally the organization to improve the customer experience (see Figure 10.3). John Hoholik led this effort, and his passion and tenacity were critical to our winning the business in an RFP pitch that started with 23 providers, including all the large BPOs. He painted a vision for the CMO and built a great relationship with him and became his trusted advisor. Once we won the business, we had to actually figure out how to deliver what we had sold. John built a cross-functional team of up-and-comers within Accent and redefined roles to help us change the paradigm. He also pushed our operational leaders well beyond their comfort zone to ensure that we delivered excellent service to complement the value-added things we were doing. As basic as it sounds, keeping the systems up, answering the phones in a timely fashion, and delivering good service were a challenge that John pushed hard on until we got it right.

| FIGURE 10.3 | Customer journey road map |

In several instances, we had to make staff changes to get this accomplished.

A significant amount of data is captured in a customer contact environment beyond the standard KPIs that can be used in leveraging big data technology to improve the customer service experience. One example of this was work we did for a large telecommunications firm, ingesting a significant sample of our call interactions with the firm's customers and mining structured and unstructured data. In a short period of time, our data scientists at GALE came up with some very interesting patterns that stimulated ideas on how to improve customer service and customer lifetime value. We were able to show which agents were best able to save defecting customers by device and tenure and how their NPS score correlated with device, tenure, and handle time of the call. This big data analysis led to a skills-based routing recommendation and optimization strategy that coincided with the client's renewed focus on customer satisfaction as a way for the client to distinguish itself in a highly competitive and promotional industry. This also positioned Accent as the client's domestic provider of choice for their best customers and a strategic thought partner.

Overcoming Transformational Challenges

Pivoting Accent was a significant transformational change, as it had been a cash cow that was milked dry by the parent company. The world changed around Accent, with its largest client drastically reducing call volume ($100+ million to $40 million for Accent) and taking a significant portion of the remaining calls offshore. The leadership at Accent was stuck in its old ways and had no support for capital infusion from the parent, and all the short-term low-cost decisions in the past about site locations and technology presented significant obstacles in creating a viable business going forward. Several of the sites were in markets where it was difficult to retain and recruit talent, and we didn't have the scale to have redundancy when impacted by bad weather, magnified by the fact that our centers were relatively geographically proximate. An investment was not made in the technology that the biggest client was mandating going forward, and we had too many system outages to be deemed reliable by clients.

The first step was to create a vision that the organization could believe in and that would lead to a viable and differentiated business. I felt that the contact center could fit into the overarching integrated customer engagement and analytics solution we were trying to develop. To create that vision and strategic plan for 2014, we established a cross-functional leadership group of some Senior Leadership Management Team members and some of their direct reports that would help develop the plan both to ensure we got the best ideas from a variety of people across the organization and also to help with buy-in from people across the company that would see it had been created very collaboratively. The exciting thing about the process is that we discovered there was great talent and enthusiasm from the level below the executive team that yearned to make Accent better and have a voice in the process.

We came up with a solid plan and made it very clear to the parent company that 2014 was a rebuilding year that was all about establishing a great business for the future and not about maximizing profitability in the short term. While we weren't given tremendous leeway in terms of financial performance or capital to invest, our decisions on technology, resources, and team structure were about creating something new in the marketplace that had been tried to be built by many others but rarely if ever had been successfully done. We intended to transform a business process outsourcer into a customer engagement agency.

We followed a key principle of evolving around the core, building upon the company's strength of having a unified view of clients' customers across multiple service touchpoints with some data analytics capabilities. It was critical to not go too far beyond the core as this would have lacked credibility with clients, and we wouldn't have been able to effectively execute and deliver value. We felt we could reasonably evolve the company with many of its current resources complemented by some new infusion of talent to develop a strong value proposition for clients that focused on using analytics to drive more personalized service interactions across multiple channels. The ability for a company to evolve and adapt, whether it is a long-established firm or a several-year-old start-up that is struggling, is absolutely critical. I see companies either get too anchored to their position or pivot so radically that it is confusing to internal and external constituents. This notion of evolving around the core has been a key principle I have followed in many situations.

We shared this vision and plan with the top 50 people in the organization in January 2014 in a two-day meeting we titled "Journey to Greatness." We held part of our meeting and our annual employee awards dinner at the Muhammad Ali Center in Louisville. The center is both beautiful and inspiring, and we felt it was a most appropriate venue to reflect upon our goal and the path we would take to get there, knowing it would require us to persevere and to overcome numerous obstacles. The team was very excited to hear about the vision and more importantly was appreciative of the transparency into the dire situation of the company based on its tenuous relationship with its top client. The people in the room were ready to dive in to face the challenges in front of us and be part of the solution of creating something unique and excellent.

While I was very excited about the buy-in and expected contribution from the broader leadership team, I knew the six-person executive team was still a large challenge. Most had been there a long time, and they were rightfully very proud of what they had built; however, they still did not recognize how ominous the situation was, because the financial performance in 2013 was still strong. It was clear a storm was brewing, but they were not willing to admit it despite the details provided by the largest client.

To gain alignment and build trust, we held an executive team meeting in Nashville, taking time to enjoy the Grand Ole Opry, live music on Broadway, and great food in one of the most exciting cities in the United States. However, the meeting itself turned ugly, with people yelling and screaming as the old regime and new guard debated the reality of our situation. I often joke that five of the six people either quit or cried in the meeting, though it was more for show than reality. There were some great tidbits from the meeting. The person who had primary responsibility for the major client thought that all was fine and that the client would come back with its tail between its legs after the Philippines "experiment" failed. Though he lived in the same city as the client, he didn't know if his client employee badge worked at the client's office. The blame game was played by client services, IT, operations, and human resources as they pointed fingers at each other as the reason why our operational delivery was so mediocre.

As we returned to Louisville, I realized that many of these functional leaders, including the heads of finance, operations, IT, client services on the biggest client, and HR, were derailing us from the path we were on by not embracing the need for change; instead they were providing headwind in our effort to transform the business. More importantly they were providing mixed signals to their teams about what needed to be done. To add to that, they weren't driving the improvement we needed in critical areas of the business to deliver consistent, adequate service levels to our clients, let alone provide the outstanding service levels we were looking to achieve. It was also clear to the organization that the executive team was dysfunctional, which led to many awkward moments in front of the team at large. So by March, I had replaced all but one of my direct reports; and other than the CFO, where I did hire an outside industry veteran, I replaced them with an up-and-coming internal candidate who was eager and ready to take on more responsibility.

As a result, we completely changed our relationship with our top client. We went from being a reactive nonfactor to being a critical thought partner that was on the front edge of its own transformation, with a new CEO being put into place by the parent company and the board. We dramatically improved the HR function, which is absolutely critical in the call center business where there is high turnover. We were able to do this by moving in Kelly Hilton who had been in marketing and had been focused on communications but had the pulse of the organization and universal respect within the company. We also steadily improved our operational delivery and the stability of our technical infrastructure, which led to better service performance. This all resulted in moving from having 8 of our 15 clients at significant risk of firing us to being able to grow broader and deeper relationships with all of them, engaging in discussions that went beyond focusing on call center KPIs such as handle time to examining their critical business matters because we had a pulse of their business and insights that they had not been privy to previously.

While it was an emotional roller coaster on multiple levels, in the end it was invigorating. I think we could have easily made Accent a $150 million business with higher EBITDA margins than a typical call center business if we had the opportunity to make a $2 million investment in technology and new site locations. However, the holding company viewed it is a nonstrategic asset and in an effort to pump up the stock price announced its intention to sell Accent at an Investor Day in December 2015. So for six months we had to finesse this news with employees and clients while we went through an extensive M&A process, deviating slightly from the policy of transparency I believe in. While I would have preferred an exit to a private equity firm that would have helped us grow the business, ultimately we sold to Startek, which had tried to create a similar model within its company for several years. The gratifying thing was how many of the Accent employees were retained in key roles at Startek after the sale.

Though I have always been a marketer, I have had responsibility for call centers at MBNA, American Express, and Harrah's/Caesars and ran a call center business as described above. As a result, I have always viewed customer care as a critical marketing channel that can build customer relationships, be a source of relevant information about the customer, and of course turn demand into revenue. Having that view changes the way these operations are run, their place in a company's hierarchy, and ultimately their value to the organization; and by taking a customer-centric approach and striving for continuity across channels, the customer experience is improved dramatically.

01110100 1110010011000010111 11100111
11 00 100011 110111101101101010 101111

Doubling Down

- **The call center and other contact channels are a valuable commodity.** They can drive revenue and brand advocacy and be a rich source of customer data.

- **Think holistically about the customer journey.** It is absolutely essential to think about the holistic customer service experience and understand the interplay among various channels.

- **Evolve around core competencies.** Even when transformational change is required, the concept of evolving around the company's core competencies is often critical to success.

Measuring Service and Driving Customer Satisfaction

I have been very fortunate to work at several companies where there were sophisticated processes to measure customer service and drive enhanced customer satisfaction. At MBNA, there were 14 key metrics that were prominently displayed in high-traffic areas of the office for everyone to see how the company was performing in service. These scores drove frontline and management bonuses, and as I described earlier, they were taken very seriously by the CEO. Above every door at MBNA appeared the statement "Think of Yourself as a Customer." The saying "brought to you by the customer" was on every paycheck.

Measuring Customer Touchpoints

Gary Loveman, the CEO of Caesars, was one of the authors of the famous *Harvard Business Review* article "The Service Profit Chain," and he instilled those principles at Harrah's. He hired a VP of customer service who had luxury hospitality experience, and each property was required to hire a customer service director to oversee service across all functions and customer touchpoints. A survey was created that had 20+ questions asking about the customer's experience across all key touchpoints, and a survey was sent each week to a sample of customers who had made a visit. We received more than 400,000 completed surveys a year, and the results drove a frontline employee bonus, 25 percent of the property management bonus, and 10 percent of the corporate bonus. Frontline employees could earn up to $200 a quarter based on achieving improvement in the percentage of A scores they received.

Both at the outset of this initiative and when times got a bit tough, some executives would argue that our investment in customer service was too significant and that employees were paid their salary to deliver a great experience without this incentive. However, we could calculate the value of improved customer service by tracking customers' survey responses and their play longitudinally (see Figure 11.1). For example, if a customer gave us a C the previous year but an A in the current year, their revenue increased by 20 percent. Conversely, if someone gave us an A the prior year but a C in the current year, their revenue decreased by 8 percent. This quantification and Gary's belief in the approach put any debate about altering the program to an end.

The details of how customers felt about each touchpoint were also used to help us identify service challenges and develop solutions to improve the guests' experience. One example of this

FIGURE 11.1	Change in revenue by change in service score

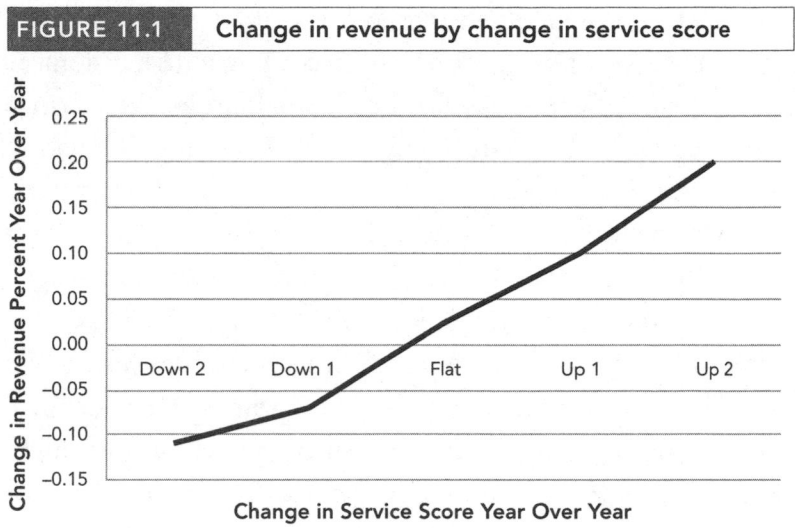

Change in Service Score Year Over Year

was the persistently low service scores we received for delivering drinks on the casino floor. Our A score in this area hovered around 35 percent across the company compared with our average score of 60 percent across other service touchpoints. The model of drink delivery was quite old school, with cocktail servers walking the floor taking orders, heading to the bar to get the drinks, then back to find the customers at their game. This often took more than 20 minutes, and cold drinks were warm and hot drinks lukewarm by the time they arrived.

Various operational improvement processes had been considered over time, but nothing seemed to work until we decided to pilot something we called beverage on demand (BoD). We developed a user-friendly interface at the slot machine to order drinks. When known customers had their Total Rewards card inserted into the slot machine, a menu would appear listing their favorite 10 drinks based on what we had seen them order in the past. Thus, it was easy for them to order their preferred beverage, and they could easily find something else if they were in the mood for something different on that day. The order went directly to the bar, and we prioritized delivery according to the customer's Total Rewards tier. Seven Stars and Diamonds got their drinks in 5 minutes, Platinum in 10 minutes, and everyone else within 20 minutes.

We started with a pilot in a couple of properties; because there were still doubters among the operators, we wanted to see the impact before fully rolling out the BoD capability. We saw our service scores increase dramatically, and we expanded BoD across all properties. This was one of several examples where detailed analytics from our customer service measurement process highlighted an opportunity to improve service delivery and made for a compelling case for change that we rallied around with an innovative solution that we effectively implemented in the operation.

Learning from the Best and the Worst

Many companies are laser-focused on delivering great service, such as Nordstrom and the Four Seasons. These companies have earned a level of loyalty from high-end customers that is admirable. Likely the company that has the most robust service delivery processes and is best known for creating a great customer experience at scale around the globe is Disney.

We spent time with Disney executives once a year for much of my time at Harrah's to share thoughts about marketing, technology, and customer service, as we felt like we were solving similar challenges though our businesses were quite different. In addition, as an annual pass holder to Disneyland for several years, I have spent more than 50 days in Disney parks and am a discerning customer.

On our info share visits, we were able to see some of the behind-the-scenes processes that Disney employs to deliver great service. And we also sat down with the Disney folks to discuss the guest experience. We talked about innovations that we were making to improve the guest experience, and Disney discussed its guest-focused innovations, including the Disney band, which has had a dramatic impact on how the guest experiences the parks. We got to participate in the highlights of the Disney Institute, where leaders from companies across the world come to learn Disney's best practices in an immersive way. The key principle for Disney is that employees must understand the company's overarching goals and how the employees contribute to fulfill those goals.

There are five pillars of business excellence according to the Disney Institute:

• Leadership

• Culture

• Customer experience

• Brand loyalty

• Creativity and innovation

On the opposite end of the spectrum in service is the domestic airline industry, as evidenced by the number of incredible stories that have been in the news in early 2017. There was dramatic reaction to the doctor who was dragged off the United flight in Chicago, losing some teeth and breaking some bones in the process. Others have been pulled off flights, endured fights with pilots, or been sent to San Francisco instead of the intended destination of Paris. From several of the airlines I fly frequently, I receive a survey after nearly every trip. There is a lot of effort and expense to track customer satisfaction, but there is something clearly lacking in their organizational processes to fundamentally create a customer-centric service culture with some airlines.

There has been a proliferation of customer feedback management platforms with companies like Medallia, Qualtrics, and Clarabridge, which help companies track customer satisfaction and interpret their results. According to Forrester, only 42 percent of companies use one or more technology solutions to support their voice-of-the-customer programs. And there seems to be limited utilization of turning insights into action to truly improve customer service.

Evolving Technology Means Evolving Service

Customer service needs to evolve in an increasingly connected and digital world. There must be a unified view of all customer interactions leveraging new technologies, and it must be proactive and anticipatory. Customers want their issue resolved in their first interaction, and worst case, they don't want to have to re-explain the situation to a new employee. Slow resolution to service issues is one of the primary contributors to customer attrition.

With the proliferation of social channels, companies need to leverage social as a service channel as a way to solve problems before the issues are shared broadly by customers through social media. Being able to resolve a problem quickly through social channels can turn a negative into a widely communicated positive very quickly. Reputation management has become critical. Negative comments can become prominent as consumers search for information about your company. Sites like Glassdoor can also be a source of negative sentiment about the company, discouraging both customers and prospective employees from engaging with you.

Measuring customer service with a significant level of granularity provides tremendous insight about the customer experience and helps identify areas for improvement. Being able to correlate improved service to increased revenue, and developing a well-constructed incentive plan, leads to great outcomes for both a company and its customers—especially when there is innovation around challenged service touchpoints that drive overall customer satisfaction with the brand.

Customer service measurement and delivery are both evolving rapidly, making it imperative that companies resolve issues quickly through a multitude of channels.

```
01110100 11100100110000101011 11100111
1100 100011 110111101101101010 101111
```

Doubling Down

- **Measure customer service at a granular level of detail.** This helps drive service improvement in a very specific and efficient way.

- **The service profit chain is not a theory.** It is a powerful motivator and value creator.

- **Innovate service through technology.** Customers rapidly embrace new technology, and as the adage goes, self-service is the best service.

- **Leverage new tools and channels.** Effectively use customer feedback platforms to identify service challenges and take action on them. You must resource effectively to control reputation management and social service channels, as they have become critical components of the customer service process.

CHAPTER

12

The Role
of Research

While my primary focus has been to create environments where sophisticated database analysis can be utilized to gain insights that can be used to develop creative solutions to improve marketing, operations, and the customer experience, I have always been a believer that research is an important complement to database analytics. Both quantitative and qualitative research can be used to validate and refine ideas for change and to help with internal syndication to overcome resistance by representing the voice of the customer. For every big initiative we did at Harrah's, we conducted research to ensure we incorporated customer feedback into our solution and had thought out the implications of our decisions. This was also an important tool to determine the best way to communicate the value proposition to customers so that they would understand and embrace the enhancements we were making to Total Rewards or some other aspect of the business.

One great example of research complementing analysis and in fact creating new insights took place in early 2009 as we were diving into the impact of the financial crisis on our business. We had analyzed our database every which way till Tuesday and presented fancy charts to our board repeatedly, showing where the revenue was declining. We knew the magnitude by level of gamer, Total Rewards tier, game type preferred, age, distance from the property, and many other factors. We knew that our VIPs had decreased their spend by 20 percent and that customers in general were spending less when they came.

However, until we did focus groups in key markets in early 2009 to understand customer perceptions, we simply felt the economy had affected us like it did everyone else in the industry based on the market numbers we could see published by the states in which we operated. The focus groups were led by a terrific moderator and strategist named Dwight Jewson, and as we talked to customers, we heard a critical perspective that had not yet hit our radar. They said the economy had affected us at Caesars more than it had them as customers, leading to a service experience far inferior to the one they had come to know and love from us. They said the property was dirtier than it had ever been, promotional offers were not as rich, the slot machines were tighter, the food wasn't as good, the employees weren't as friendly, and some of their favorite employees were no longer there.

The reality is that the customers were right, as we had cut our labor dramatically to match the fall in revenue and we were managing our expenses tightly. The challenge was that the guest visitation levels were virtually flat, so the operational stress on the properties was still the same; it was just that customers were spending less and that a lower-value customer could now get in at a less expensive rate. We had scaled back offers both to reflect the decrease in customer play and even more so to try to tie marketing spend to incremental customer behavior, and we did reduce the customer payout on slot machines to bring more to the bottom line. Customers felt their gaming spend was more precious now and expected more appreciation from us.

Alarmed by the findings from the focus groups, we decided to invest in a significant quantitative survey in which we connected with 20,000 Total Rewards members purposely with varying play levels across our key markets and 10,000 nonmembers in order to talk to a broader customer base. In the survey we asked about their entire travel and entertainment spend, as one of our objectives was to find new sources of revenue to offset the decline we were seeing from our best customers. While we were able to categorize responders into 11 strategic segments to better think about pockets of potential, the most disconcerting discovery was that for our VIPs, gaming had moved well down their list of travel and entertainment activities that were important to them. While they said they would continue to reduce their gaming spend 20 percent from historical levels, they made it clear that other forms of leisure spend were more important to them and that they would use more of their declining discretionary spend on things such as family trips, sports tickets, shopping, and golf memberships. In essence, their risk profile had changed after the economic crisis, and they were going to be more prudent with their gaming spend, limiting themselves to a per-trip budget even if it expired more quickly on an unlucky visit.

The research clearly had our attention, and we very quickly organized a cross-functional task force of a dozen core members from across the company and led by my VP of VIP marketing, Brett Kline. We had done several initiatives to transform the world of VIP hosted marketing with a small group of VIP leaders in our major markets with tremendous success. As we organized the task force, Gary Loveman provided terrific advice and suggested that we include several smart people who hadn't really lived and breathed VIP marketing before to get a fresh perspective. This allowed us to add a half-dozen very smart people into the mix who had various functional responsibilities across the enterprise, creating an internal "dream team" whose task was to figure out how to recapture a portion of the $300+ million of VIP revenue we had lost since September 2008.

The team dived into the research to set our baseline understanding of the situation, and we conducted deep analysis of our database to help uncover areas of opportunities. We knew we couldn't solve all the issues in a fiscally responsible way, but we did endeavor to fix the biggest pain points in the service experience for our best guests. Service measurement was critical for us, and as part of our process we received nearly half a million customer service surveys back a year in which customers provided feedback on more than 20 dimensions of their experience with us. Our statisticians did complex analysis and showed that there were a couple of key touchpoints that had more significant weight in the overall experience, which we knew led to higher LTV. The task force developed manual and technology-enabled solutions to enhance these key touchpoints that we syndicated to the Operations Committee and got approval to implement.

A critical finding was that if a VIP customer had a host, there was a premium in the customer's service score compared with those that didn't have a host. More importantly, if the host actually had interacted with the player on that particular trip, the service premium was quite dramatic. This led to an even more radical and costly recommendation that the team felt was financially justified. In 2003, we required our 900 VIP hosts to spend one day a week calling customers they didn't know very well—new, nonloyal, or defectors—and the hosts' bonus was based on them growing the revenue of their specific customer portfolio. This had worked exceptionally well and fueled 20+ percent annual growth through August 2008.

Given that we had cut property labor, we believed that we should reduce the number of customers a host had from 1,000 to 400 and have the hosts entirely focus on service, ensuring their customers' needs were met before and during their visits to us. To fill the gap of the hosts' sales role, we determined that we had to hire true hunters and create a real sales function that found new customers. We hired a recruiting firm, a training firm, and a sales consultant by the name of Dan Weinfurter to help ensure that we built out a world-class sales function; and then we hired more than 100 new people that would look for new customers. We infused these capabilities within our group meeting function as well, as there was some impact created by President Obama suggesting companies, particularly banks, should not have meetings in Las Vegas, and this had made life challenging for a period of time in filling our meeting space.

What the example above shows is how effectively analytics and research can coexist in an iterative fashion. Our analytics told us there was a problem that we needed to explore with our guests, and in turn our research led us to do a deeper dive analytically in a focused way to create solutions. Before we implemented the solutions, we validated them with customers, measuring the impact and customer reaction to the proposed changes.

Research Is a Critical Tool for Gaining Insight About Longstanding Beliefs

We have seen research be a critical tool with many of our GALE clients, in some instances helping refute longstanding beliefs that have been held in the company.

Just a few examples:

• For one retailer that was considering building a loyalty program, customers indicated that a standard points-and-rewards program was much less important to them than getting early access to the latest fashions or first access to distressed inventory discount sales.

• For another retail organization whose view from the top was that customers always had time to explore in the physical store, we were able to quantify what percentage of customers are time constrained and doing their exploration online and via mobile and planning their store visit, which helped validate an omnichannel vision.

• For the CPG manufacturer that *invented* the juice cleanse category, we diagnosed a root cause of declining sales in the direct-to-consumer online sales model that originally propelled them to success. While brand managers were focused on the product ordering UX and search engine optimization, we found that consumers' channel preferences for the category were shifting irreversibly to physical retail. It was time to turn more attention to winning shelf space.

• For a technology solution provider, we leveraged consumer research to help understand that the company's competition was much broader than just other tech companies. Just as it is for almost everyone else, Amazon is the major threat to the company's success.

Having a ready panel of consumers has been a critical part of our success to complement traditional research methods used with clients' known customers. Rapid-cycle research provides strategic insights that build credibility when pitching or selling an idea to an organization and can challenge longstanding internal beliefs. As noted in an earlier chapter, we call this solution "Ask GALE," which is a global panel of more than 5 million people with a diverse makeup that enables us to pick the appropriate audience for the client. Ask GALE is a suite of primary research tools that incorporate the voice of the customer and empowers brands to make critical business decisions with confidence. These include the global panel, online surveys, user testing, quantitative online discussion boards, social listening, and immersive participatory research. The results have been very beneficial in a variety of scenarios including helping us to be informed for client pitches and often to be armed with a provocative insight that stimulates constructive debate in those meetings.

An example of this is a recent RFP process we participated in for a global brand; we had garnered some insights about the brand that we presented at the final pitch meeting, and this proved critical to our winning the business. The assignment was to help the company more effectively sell a new category of product, as the company was not seeing the results it wanted. Our research provided interesting insights about what both motivates and concerns people about the category at large and at what magnitude, and those findings informed our proposed communication approach as well as showed that we were taking a consumer-centric and strategic approach to one of the company's core business challenges.

Even in a sophisticated analytical environment, consumer research is an important component in understanding the story and the opportunities. Often an iterative approach between analysis and research leads to the best outcomes, as research can help explain the why behind customer patterns, and it can provide direction on where to dig deeper analytically. Validating the proposed path forward from analytic insights with consumers before going live invariably leads to tweaks that will make the proposed changes better.

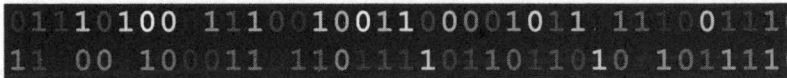

Doubling Down

- **Customer research and robust analytics are highly complementary.** Used iteratively, they can lead to creating innovative solutions that will be adopted well by customers.

- **Customer research can be very provocative.** Often it can be a starting point to drive transformational change.

- **Have a consumer panel at your disposal.** Having customers you can reach out to quickly is an invaluable research tool.

Brand and Advertising Measurement and the Explosion of Digital Media

The well-known adage of "I know half of my advertising is working but I am not sure which half" still rings true for many companies when it comes to traditional advertising. TV advertising is a multibillion dollar business and will continue to be, even with the increasing penetration of watching shows on a variety of platforms; however, it is shocking that big brands aren't more scientific about their spend so they can make more informed marketing mix decisions given how measurable CRM, digital, and social are.

Quantifying Advertising Returns

At Caesars, we had to fight hard for traditional advertising dollars, money that came from the property budgets, primarily because our CRM and digital advertising were measurable in a very refined way that enabled us to optimize spend in those categories. In addition, brand was perceived to be much less important a pillar to our success than loyalty, service, gaming product, and other amenities such as dining and entertainment. Our traditional advertising budget was cut in half during the budgeting process in 2009 after the economic crisis from a relatively small base of spend, given that we were supporting 14 brands and nearly 40 properties in 15 major cities including some of the most expense advertising markets in the country.

In 2010, we developed a new brand campaign for Caesars that we were very happy with, and we believed it would have a significant impact on brand perception, which had taken a bit of a hit with new multibillion dollar competitors having opened in Las Vegas. However, we were struggling to get the budget from the Las Vegas operations team to properly launch this great new campaign. The digital advertising budget was centrally controlled, though clearly we were accountable for driving a significant number of room nights and a material amount of revenue. However, we felt like the last million dollars of our digital budget was not going to drive a material return on ad spend, given the suppressed room rates that we were experiencing at the time, so we decided to reallocate that money to traditional advertising to support the new Caesars campaign.

We wanted to track the impact of the TV, print, and outdoor campaign we had planned in an attempt to secure more budget for the following year, keeping in mind this was not direct response TV advertising but rather a brand-building campaign with a modest call to action at the end of the spot. We decided we would run the Caesars campaign in Los Angeles, as the booking window from that market into Las Vegas is relatively short. To measure the results, we looked at a variety of factors including calls into the reservations center from the LA DMA (designated market area), hits to the website, and visitation and revenue from LA customers. We compared those results with how Caesars performed in other proximate markets such as San Diego, San Francisco, and Phoenix and also compared the results with how our other Vegas properties were performing year over year in LA.

Ultimately we could quantify the return on the traditional advertising as we saw a nice lift in revenue for Caesars in LA. There were more direct bookings and a meaningful shift down in the percentage of rooms going to online travel agencies like Expedia and Travelocity, which typically were lower margin. This led us to allocate more budget to traditional advertising the following year and start building back the brand perceptions of Caesars.

Measuring brand health was extremely important to us, and we felt like it was important to monitor trends longitudinally. While awareness of the Caesars brand was nearly universal and the perception was positive, in early 2009 we could see that the guest satisfaction with the Caesars brand was declining at a high rate, and it was much lower than other luxury properties in its competitive set, as shown in Table 13.1.

TABLE 13.1	Awareness for Caesars was high but satisfaction levels had dropped					
	Satisfaction					
Property (base sizes for 2009 data	August 2006	May 2007	February 2008	April 2009	Change from 2008 to 2009	Change from 2006 to 2009
Venetian (n = 220)	70%	70%	72%	72%	0	2
Ceasars Palace (n = 257)	61%	64%	67%	55%	−12	−6
Bellagio (n = 257)	70%	71%	75%	72%	−3	2
Wynn (n = 146)	54%	66%	69%	61%	−8	7

We wanted to peel back the onion on what was driving this decline in satisfaction scores. One thing we saw as we dived into the data was that satisfaction and perception of Caesars varied dramatically depending on whether you stayed in one of the three newer hotel towers as opposed to one of the two older ones. The rooms in the older part of the casino hadn't been renovated in more than a decade and were just over 300 square feet and genuinely were a very mediocre hotel experience. They were certainly not luxury rooms and definitely not Caesars-worthy, as evidenced by all the 1s and 2s in the Centurion and Roman tower columns in Table 13.2.

As any observer of NPS or the service profit chain would predict, these low-satisfaction scores for those who stayed in the older rooms led to lower revenue, as those customers did not return to stay at Caesars at the same rate as the customers who had stayed in the better rooms. While they may have loved Caesars, they couldn't risk being stuck in one of the old rooms and likely booked at one of the competitors that had a more universally

TABLE 13.2	The Centurion and Roman Towers don't live up to Caesars' room experience, leading to lower satisfaction (based on a 5 point scale)				

	Palace	Augustus	Forum	Centurion	Roman
Overal	5	5	4.5	2	2
Brand Elements					
Bold	5	5	5	2	2
World-Renown	4	4	4	1.5	1
Attentive	4	4	5	2	1
Color Palette	4.5	4.5	3.5	3	2
Layout	5	5	5	2	2
Elevators	5	5	2	2	2
Corridors	5	5	3	2	2
Lighting	3	3	4	2	3
Furniture	5	5	5	2	2
Bed/Bedding	5	5	5	2	2
Finishes/Fixtures	5	5	5	2	2
Bathroom	5	5	5	2	1
Technology	3	3	4	1	2

great room product. Thus, we could quantify the impact of subpar rooms and how significantly they were taking away from the perception of and affinity for the greatest brand in gaming.

We knew we had to do something about this situation, but in our postrecession environment, we knew that capital was tight and that getting approval for a room renovation would be difficult.

Leveraging Analytic Insights to Sustain and Build Audience

Simultaneous to dealing with the room issue, we wanted to improve a poor retail experience in the heart of the casino that housed stores selling statues and uninspiring clothes and jewelry. After contemplating several ideas, we became very excited about partnering with Nobu to build a large, beautiful restaurant and to create the first Nobu hotel in the world by converting one of the old towers to a new experience. We did research on the Nobu brand, and we felt like it would attract a new audience—between the older core gamer and the young Pure nightclub crowd—that would be very profitable. We also had seen in the brand health report that Caesars Palace was slipping in some key categories that define luxury, such as upscale and stylish, as shown in Table 13.3.

TABLE 13.3	Brand Health Tracker: We were losing the luxury battle to Bellagio, Venetian, Wynn			
	Ceasars Palace	Bellagio	Venetian	Wynn
Upscale	52%	84%	82%	94%
Stylish	40%	73%	80%	90%
Tasteful	35%	72%	71%	74%
Sophisticated	34%	65%	68%	92%
Hip and Cool	23%	39%	42%	57%

As we learned more about the Nobu brand, we discovered that it was particularly strong in the areas where Caesars Palace was weak compared with its luxury competitive set (see Table 13.4).

Now that we had our desired path and story, we had to sell it to the board. With all the insight from above, everyone agreed we needed to make a change, including potentially shutting down one of the old towers, and this was discussed as an option in the board meeting. There was some consternation about blending the Asian-themed Nobu with the Roman Caesars brand and some hesitance about building the first Nobu hotel, but ultimately we got agreement to move forward. David Rockwell was selected to

TABLE 13.4	**Top Nobu traits where Ceasars Palace were weak**

NOBU HOTEL
CAESARS PALACE

	Nobu
Upscale	57%
Hip and Cool	40%
Stylish	40%
Modern	39%
Tasteful	36%
Sophisticated	35%

design the rooms, and he did so in an elegant yet prudent manner—and the PR buzz was significant.

We used similar logic to gain support for additional capital projects throughout Caesars Palace to keep it relevant in the luxury category. These included a world-class spa, renovations to the pool, a brand-new buffet concept, and changes in our restaurant partners. The whole process started with deep analytics insights at the intersection of product and customer to quantify the financial impact.

The Explosion of Digital Media

The need to understand the returns of digital media has become more important because of the explosive growth of digital media and its acute measurability. Here are some eye-opening 2016 stats from the Interactive Advertising Bureau as reported in *Ad Age* in April 2017:

- Digital advertising grew by 22 percent in 2016 and amounted to $72.5 billion in the United States.

- For the first time, more was spent on digital advertising than TV advertising, with digital amounting to $71.3 billion in 2016 in the United States.

- eMarketer estimated that $25 billion of the digital advertising in 2016 was programmatic.

- Digital video accounted for $9.1 billion of digital spend, and $4.2 billion of that video spend was on mobile devices.

- Social media advertising grew to $16.3 billion in 2016, and digital radio advertising grew to $1.1 billion.

At GALE, we have leveraged our big data environment to help several clients optimize their traditional advertising spend. We ingest a variety of data including sales by store and channel, call center and website metrics, and a wide set of external data to determine an enhanced media allocation by market and channel. In addition, while initially we didn't plan to execute digital media, we have built a robust capability in this area both because our clients were asking for our help and because we found it was a natural extension of our data-driven CRM and digital work with them. We are now able to help clients manage customers in a sophisticated and cohesive way from the top of the funnel in digital media through the transaction and in-venue experience.

While the promise of media mix optimization has been present for several years, it seems like it is still in its infancy despite advances in technology. One of the reasons for this is that marketing budgets still reside in functional silos, and moving those budgets across channels and product lines is not part of many companies' process. However, it is critical that effort be made to evaluate traditional marketing spend, given how significant the expense is and given the accurate measurability of digital and CRM channels.

01110100 1110 10011 0001011 11 0111
11 00 100011 11011110110110 101111

Doubling Down

- **You need a solution to measure your return on advertising investment.** With the detailed measurability of digital advertising, there will be increased pressure to measure the returns of traditional advertising.

- **Invest in brand health metrics.** They can have significant strategic and long-term implications for the business, highlighting your performance relative to that of competitors.

- **New media channels are surpassing TV.** Digital advertising spend topped TV spend for the first time in 2016, and video, social media advertising, and digital radio are all becoming meaningful in the advertising mix.

- **Marketing optimization tools are still nascent.** The adoption and use of channel optimization tools has happened much more slowly than would be expected.

Leadership

Leadership is absolutely critical to achieve a customer-centric and analytically driven culture. The CEO of the organization must embrace this approach and challenge the status quo by asking questions and seeking data-informed arguments and recommendations. As well, the CEO must be willing to find the balance between having business unit or brand autonomy and a centralized function that builds capabilities that drive change with equal authority to the operators. Too often, I have seen companies that want their "corporate" function to be a shared services order taker for the business units, and I am constantly surprised how many CEOs don't embrace a customer-centric approach other than at the highest level of pushing for good service for all.

There are many people and events that have influenced my leadership style and approach to creating great teams. I was very fortunate to have a great boss in Paul Muller as I came out of the management development program at MBNA to start my career. Paul was an experienced executive with vast knowledge of the banking industry and how to develop great teams. In addition to his great intellect, Paul had a warm yet demanding approach that inspired those that worked for him to do their best work. He was very supportive, yet expected more in a positive way, but also gave an appropriate amount of space to learn and explore on your own.

It is often the small things that make a difference from a leadership perspective. I recall when I was making my first appearance presenting to the senior executive team at American Express, Al Kelly took the time to write down the names and titles of all the people in the room so I would know who they were. It demonstrated an awareness of my circumstance in a critical meeting that increased my comfort level.

There is no doubt I transformed into a senior executive during my time at Harrah's as my opportunities and responsibilities grew, and there were many lessons learned along the way, including some painful ones. You must get comfortable in your own skin and demonstrate confidence when presenting in senior forums or when inspiring a team, and you need to do it displaying a measured balance of passion and expertise.

Adversity as an Opportunity for Leadership Growth

One of the most painful moments in my career took place at the "Happiest Place on Earth" at a marketing offsite meeting for 100 people in the fall of 2003. Within a year of my being promoted to SVP, Gary announced in front of this group that he was going to split corporate marketing: I was to run Loyalty/Retention Marketing, and a divisional colleague would run Brand/ Acquisition Marketing. I thought this was a flawed structure and suboptimal for both the organization at large and me personally. Gary's rationale was that he wanted me to focus on the harder problems and bigger opportunities, though I certainly took it as a slap in the face and felt it was unjust. It was also disappointing that my closest colleague, Amanda Totaro, quit on the spot because of the change in her reporting structure, though I was very supportive of her decision.

While I was certainly pissed, I reflected upon what I needed to do to get better as an executive. I explored executive education programs, and I enrolled in one run by Columbia University called High Impact Leadership. As part of the program, I had to solicit feedback on a broad array of factors from a wide range of people I worked with, including my boss, peers, direct reports, and internal and external constituents. The feedback report was quite extensive, not to mention eye-opening, and during the intense one-week course, there were a series of workshops that helped me address areas where I needed to improve. It truly was one of the seminal experiences in my career.

Gary also challenged me to think about making changes to my direct reports, despite the fact we had started to receive numerous accolades for our marketing abilities and accomplishments. Many of my direct reports had grown up in gaming and had come to corporate from property roles, which was a beneficial complement to my external noncasino background at the outset. This helped ensure that our new initiatives could be feasibly executed at the property level. However, these direct reports were neither giving me the scale needed to cover the multitude of things on my plate nor driving innovation within their function. As a result, we sent many of them back to operational roles and hired new direct reports from outside the industry. Several had consulting experience from Bain or McKinsey, and others came from great brands in other industries. The focus was on finding smart, analytically inquisitive people who could drive innovation and change collaboratively with the field while learning the casino industry. This was a dramatic shift that spurred our next wave of cutting-edge capabilities. The impact on the business was significant, including dramatically enhancing our digital expertise, launching interactive CRM, engaging in domestic Asian marketing, and taking on several other key projects

Organizational Design Trade-Offs

In late 2009 I had to go through the same type of turnover with my direct reports. The world had changed around us after the economic crisis, and several of my folks just couldn't evolve to drive the innovation we needed. One example was in our sales function, which acted more like a client services function than sales organization since their primary role historically was about keeping our best customers happy. However, with such significant revenue decline from our best customers, we needed true hunters to find new customers, and the leader of that group was not a sales expert.

Similarly, multicultural marketing had concentrated primarily on domestic Asians for the first few years, with a focus on gamers. We needed to make a push into targeting Hispanics to drive more volume, and the leader of that area wasn't equipped to strategically drive this evolution.

Finally, our retail store function had been very successful, with impressive margins on a $150 million business. However, the retail experience in Las Vegas had become a sea of sameness, with the top luxury brands, jewelry, and logo merchandise dominating and present at every casino. Status quo was not going to drive traffic or steal share, and I felt that significant innovation was required; this was met with deep resistance from the leader of that group, and we parted ways. I took his number two and had her run the core operations, and I drove retail innovation, partnering with external retail experts. From that work concepts were born, such as the Grand Bazaar in front of Bally's in Las Vegas, the Viking Cooking School in Atlantic City, and several other cool ideas that did not get to the goal line, generally because of the lack of available capital budget.

With organizational design, there are always trade-offs when exploring options that are in the consideration set. Often it comes down to weighing the optimal design against the skill sets of the people that are in place and realizing the breadth and depth that direct reports can handle. We all want more boxes in our org chart, a fancier title, and more authority, but there are occasions when focus on a hard problem is required even when it means a more narrowly defined role.

It's never easy giving people tough feedback or, of course, determining that the best path is for them to "pursue other opportunities." It is critical to have strong HR processes in place to evaluate the team through collaborative talent reviews, where performance rating scores are debated by peers to ensure there is equity and also to ensure that people are given the proper feedback. In any organization, 5 to 10 percent of the people will be in a "needs improvement/unsatisfactory" category. These employees will need to be aggressively managed to improve—and if that fails, they must be moved out. Developing detailed and measurable action plans for people in this category is essential, so that they know what they need to do. Just as important, it is vital to have documented evidence for legal protection if they decide to be litigious when they are dismissed. Conversely, ensuring that "stars" are nurtured and given new opportunities and shown appreciation is critical to retain and grow top talent. As long as these processes have been followed and the communication has been open through dialogue and written documentation, one can feel better about removing someone from a position when it is what is needed for the greater good of the company.

Learning from One's Colleagues

Observing the strengths and weaknesses of your boss and other senior leaders in your organization is an important development opportunity. I mentioned how important Paul Muller was early in my career as my first boss out of college.

The person I worked with for the longest time was Gary Loveman, as we were together at Harrah's and Caesars for 12 years. His intellect, analytic orientation, incredible public speaking skills, and desire for greatness were all attributes I appreciated. The fact that he both gave me an enormous opportunity to work on a multitude of things and had such high expectations pushed me and the team around me to incredible heights. People often ask if it was intimidating to work for such a marketing savant. For me, I knew the expectations and held myself to the same high standards, beating myself up for things that we could do better, even if not fully in my control. I also observed some things that could be better, including the ability to stimulate dialogue and debate to get to the best answer or at least create a mechanism for people to feel part of the decision-making process.

I give Gary credit for bringing in a former Harvard colleague of his to work with the senior management team to examine how decisions were made, which typically was top-down without much discussion. It forced self-reflection and a feeling of vulnerability for Gary, but ultimately his willingness to go through this personally made us a more cohesive senior management team and a more collaborative decision-making process became the norm. I also recognized the need to understand organizational dynamics, giving consideration to how different constituents would react to change, truly putting myself in their shoes to make sure a planned course was the right one or at least would be communicated properly so people could understand the logic of decisions.

There were also many things I admired about Gary's predecessor, Phil Satre. The way he connected with the frontline employees at the property level in a warm and genuine way was phenomenal to observe, and it was easy to see how much it meant to the people he interacted with.

I have seen some interesting behavior from several folks I have worked with over the years, including the screamers and those who throw things in frustration in meetings. One of the funnier things happened at a company that did frequent off-sites in a beautiful rural setting. PowerPoint was prohibited, but that didn't necessarily foster more dialogue or innovation, as people spent many hours writing detailed financials on flip charts in advance of the meeting and brought up large binders to accompany those charts when it was their turn to present in order to be prepared for any detailed question. It was comical to see people juggle stacks of paper with markers in a game of physical and mental dexterity as the CEO tried to embarrass them with very detailed questions that were more times than not innocuous.

I have also seen a very successful entrepreneur and deal maker whose big personality had enabled him to establish a great business. However, he wasn't able to alter his style to have more substantive conversations when that was required from the senior clients (often CEOs) around the table, always gravitating to discussing his material possessions and celebrity interactions. An important element of leadership is the ability to adapt your behavior to the situation.

While the primary focus of this book is about how to use data to improve marketing and the customer experience to drive higher profitability and customer satisfaction, I have seen how important leadership is to rally an organization around these capabilities. To drive transformational change and create an analytic culture, the CEO must stress the importance of it and inspire the organization to believe in the journey. It also takes a strong-willed yet collaborative leader who is responsible for this effort day to day for it have a chance to be successful. Driving transformational change is extremely hard, and it requires persistence and resilience because people naturally will reject change. I often say that the transformational leader needs to be able to get off the mat often, as this person will be punched in the gut numerous times along the way. Bouncing back quickly is paramount, as is having a CEO providing air cover to increase an organization's customer centricity and analytic focus.

As a CMO or other senior functional leader, you need to develop your skills as you evolve from contributor to executive. Periodically investing the time to reflect upon what you do well and what can be improved is paramount. Whether it is with annual employee surveys or a focused program, leadership growth is essential.

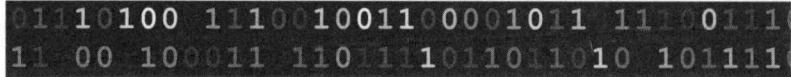

Doubling Down

- **Learn from adversity.** Facing adversity can be a great learning experience. In order to scale and to become an effective leader, you need to feel comfortable not only in delegating, but also in being challenged.

- **Org design is not an exact science.** Do the best to match the people you have with the optimal functional structure; the most critical thing is to strive for clarity in roles and responsibilities while also building a team culture.

- **Observe and learn from other leaders.** Then make it your own!

PART 3

The Proliferation of Digital and Big Data

Digital Defined

For being such a pervasive part of our lives, digital is a term that is often misused. Some people think it only entails websites, while others realize that it enables immediate communication across multiple channels including mobile. This confusion permeates the agency world, with most agencies claiming they have digital expertise when they have no capability to build technically oriented digital solutions that improve the customer experience. To clarify what most agencies do from what we do at GALE, we often talk about the difference between digital communication, which is focused on upper-funnel activity, and digital marketing, which is focused on lower-funnel conversion.

At GALE, our digital expertise is focused on being able to use data to create relevant real-time communication with customers. Generally the objective is to drive a purchase; thus, we are more interested in lower-funnel activities.

Harrahs.com

When we built harrahs.com in 1999 when digital was just emerging as an important channel, we decided to build one web platform for all 16 properties we had at the time. We did this for two main reasons. First, we wanted to drive scale with the technical integration we planned to do with the data warehouse. Second, we didn't expect that there would be digital expertise at all our property locations. Critical and sophisticated areas of the site that were universal included booking customer-specific hotel offers or yielded rates based on projections from the revenue management system and seeing personalized Total Rewards offers received through direct mail. Each property had common pages about promotions, entertainment, and restaurants that not only were easy for the properties to update through the content management system but also provided consistency for website visitors as they explored various markets.

This model persisted as we expanded significantly through acquisitions, including having more than 12 casino brands. While there was debate from brand zealots about whether we were hurting the Caesars and Horseshoe brands by including them on harrahs.com, in addition to the cost consideration, we knew that consumers shop across brands and markets as part of their decision-making process; this is why travel sites like Expedia, Kayak, and others do so well. We wanted to give our customers choice when they were making a reservation in Las Vegas or the other markets where we had multiple properties, whether that was to go more upscale with the brand or room type or to be more judicious with the hotel spend so they could save their money for other entertainment choices when they arrived. In fact, we saw that more than 20 percent of the time, customers chose to book at a property other than the one they started with when seeking room rates.

Digital transformation is something we at GALE have been working on with a large CPG client for several years, and we have come to realize it is a significant change management initiative. Like most CPGs, the client has many brands that are run autonomously, and they each had their own websites running on various platforms with an array of minimal functionality. Also, having only a limited amount of direct-to-consumer business and being reliant on selling its product through retailers, the client didn't know much about its actual customers.

We painted a vision for becoming a digital and customer-centric organization over time to help our client build relationships with customers and steal more share. We started with a beautiful-lifestyle "corporate" site as a way to start building relationships with customers. The site was visually beautiful and provided dynamic content, and it attracted interest from several of the key brands in the company that wanted a site that looked just as nice. However, we had a bigger purpose in mind; we wanted to track individuals who visited the multiple brands—track what they were doing on the site and ask them relevant questions about their shopping behaviors. The synergy of having these multiple sites running on our unchained content management platform and tracking the data in our Alchemy big data environment has been quite powerful, as we are able to continuously update our profile of individual visitors and present more relevant content the next time they visit any of the sites, providing us with the opportunity of cross-selling within and across brands. We can build upon this with the emails we now send for the various brands as well.

Digital should be an important tool even for those companies that have relatively infrequent interactions with their customers because they are selling big-ticket items. We worked on a pitch for a large producer of kitchen and laundry appliances that is generally disaggregated from the shopping experience because the product is sold at Lowe's, Home Depot, other big-box retailers, and mom-and-pop stores. To us the opportunity and the challenge boiled down to the question of how could the brand be more integral during the exploration and purchase process and even beyond.

It started with thinking about the consumers and their journey in the product category, which we validated and quantified with our Ask GALE research panel. We learned how different the emotional mindset is if you are buying one of these appliances because your existing one stopped working suddenly as opposed to if you are doing a kitchen remodel or buying a new home. The former is characterized by a frantic state of how am I going to keep the household running if I can't cook dinner or wash clothes, and there is an urgency to make a decision. The latter represents a more optimistic and reflective state as you contemplate your dream kitchen or laundry room. Understanding what journey the prospective customer is on is a critical first step that can be determined as the person interacts with the website.

This ASK GALE survey also confirmed that consumers were overwhelmed by a sea of sameness for each of these appliance products, and it was hard to distinguish features and benefits across price points in addition to the various visual options available. With a quantified understanding of this pain point in the consumer journey, we ideated a digital solution to help people get to the right decision for them and to leverage mobile to be able to find their top choices no matter what retailer they went to. By building an inherently useful mobile tool, that was also visually stunning, and happened to guide consumers to our client's brand and products, we aimed to keep consumers committed to the brand and not be influenced by the store employee who might have a financial incentive to sell another brand or might lead the consumer in a different direction based on his or her knowledge of another brand. Digital, and especially mobile, can be a critical way for brands to have a voice at the moment of purchase in a store environment it did not control.

We also observed and heard from customers that the registration process was quite cumbersome. Again we felt like there was a digital solution to facilitate this and capture valuable information about the customer. We also learned that consumers only use a fraction of the technology in these appliances, whether it is always using the same setting for their dishwasher or washing machine or not achieving their cooking prowess with the stove or oven they had just purchased. While keeping the family running smoothly was the most important goal for the majority of the brand's target customers, there was appeal to the notion of impressing friends with not only the look of the kitchen but the meals that the person could now prepare. We believed that interacting with recent buyers by educating them on their new product and giving them recipe ideas was a great way for the brand to stay engaged with the customer and build loyalty that would drive social advocacy in the short term and repurchase down the road even if it was several years away. We also felt there was an opportunity to drive direct ancillary revenue by making it easy to subscribe to reorder either complementary items such as laundry detergent or cooking utensils or replacement items such as filters.

We see the same opportunity to more fully leverage digital for our automobile client as a relevant way to stay engaged with the customer in between the several-year cycle of buying a new car. With connected platforms, it should be easy to know what service is needed when and inform the owner proactively. Engaging with the brand through partners and sponsored events can also build deeper brand equity.

Too often, people think of digital as a website. As technology has evolved and customers interact with brands differently, digital has come to have a much broader definition. Being a digitally driven organization means that you can interact with customers in a contextually relevant way in near real time no matter where the customers are or what device they are using. It provides a unifying and gratifying experience for customers that builds loyalty and paves the way for sustainable success.

Impact of Big Data

I t is amazing how much technology has evolved in the last few years, enabling all the things we accomplished at Harrah's and Caesars to be done more quickly and effectively. Big data is a popular buzz phrase much like CRM was 10 to 15 years ago, but I think many companies have gotten wrapped around the axle about what it means and how it can positively impact their business. Significant quantities of structured and unstructured data can be mined by the machine and interpreted by data scientists very quickly to create insights that weren't previously possible; however, the right talent and processes must be in place to harness it.

Stats on Big Data

Technologies such as Hadoop and Spark have been implemented broadly and enable businesses to process large quantities of data quickly to create insights. There has been a significant increase in unstructured and schemeless databases, and the success of Amazon's web services has led to new entrants from Google and Microsoft. A survey done by Tableau, a top business intelligence tool company, showed that 78 percent of the firms that responded said they would be doing more with Hadoop in the next 12 months compared with only 3 percent that said they would be doing less.

Companies can gather a plethora of information from a variety of sources, but it is critical that they have the right analytical resources to leverage it and take action in a practical way for the business. That could be to improve personalization in marketing, create an enhanced experience in the "store" environment, or have a better understanding of business performance. It is critical to partner data scientists with business strategists to help interpret the results from the machine and create meaningful insights. Understanding the business and opportunities will lead to more productive output when combined with the machine-driven learnings since there will be more context.

Microclustering

Many of our client engagements at GALE start with microclustering, which entails gathering data from disparate clients' systems into our big data environment that runs on the Amazon cloud. We take in demographic info, transactional data for the last several years, and as much behavioral data as we can, including web logs, to create views of the customer that the client has not previously seen, as it has not been able to aggregate the data internally. Depending on the depth of the data and complexity of the business, we generate anywhere between 40 and 80 microclusters with unique performance characteristics that make it clear how to treat each differently to positively influence behavior. Clearly we see dramatic differences in purchase behavior, profitability, and depth of engagement, but many of the features and the description of the cluster make it clear what behavior you want to change from the group. That could be moving nonlodgers to lodgers in hospitality or migrating a retail customer from online to one who shops in store as well. Clusters are created in a very iterative process between the machine, data scientists, GALE business strategists, the client marketing team, and, if there is one, a data science person or team. Adding business context and understanding the opportunity to personalize will make the clusters relevant and actionable.

With the microcluster output, we create a business case that details the size of the prize of engaging in a more robust CRM and loyalty process, built up by cluster, leveraging both past migrations the company had experienced and a predictive view based on our analysis and models. The business case is used both to build momentum among the senior team for the need for change and to justify any investment required to capture the opportunity.

Our focus with developing microclusters is to ensure that the client can execute against them in a reasonable way. So while we may present 40 to 80 microclusters, we will highlight the lowest-hanging fruit and often suggest clients start doing something more personalized for three to five of the clusters to start with, realizing there is an executional burden of having more versions of email or direct mail or more content on the website or messaging in store. The depth and breadth of sophistication can increase over time as the results justify the investment to add more people or to automate technology.

Programmatic Content

Microclustering facilitates what we call programmatic content. Of course, programmatic media has become critical in the advertising arena as a way to drive very productive use of media dollars and is well understood. What we mean by programmatic content is the ability to deliver the right message to customers at the right time irrespective of channel. This could be publishing the most relevant recipe on a food website or sending an email about a performer that the customer would be interested in who is coming to a nearby venue. It is all about being able to anticipate the customers' desires and needs and hitting them with the right message.

Big Data Capabilities

One of the powers of big data is the ability to integrate data from a variety of sources to create views of the customer that clients haven't seen previously. That can be transactional data, unstructured call center outcomes, web browsing history, and information from third-party sources. This data is often held in various data environments, and the ability to process this much data quickly is how the magic occurs.

Our big data capabilities were on full display in a project where we helped an integrated resort validate its proposed revenue projections that enabled it to win the ability to do the project and helped it determine how to optimize the marketing expense to maximize profitability when achieving that target. We dived into data from the client's markets and created look-alike models while keeping in mind the similarities and differences of the markets. With third-party data we estimated unconstrained demand and predicted what revenue and share the client would expect to capture by a 60+ zone approach based on the zone's demographics and proximity to competitors. We also determined the relative reinvestment amount and type that would be required based on the competitive layout of the market. At a higher level, we helped the client think through how revenue would be distributed across various customer segments and what tactics to use to capture that revenue with relative priority.

The output of this work was used by the resort to develop its detailed budget as the opening for the property approached, and it gave the resort confidence that the revenue target was aggressive but achievable with the right plan. Since the property opened, analysis has been conducted regularly to pinpoint how the revenue is being achieved by zone to determine what dials should be modified. Also, customers are scored based on the zone approach, enabling CRM execution to be much more efficient in addition to being more automated from an execution perspective.

Another interesting big data–led project was for a loyalty platform fintech that is focused on local financial institutions and merchants. The company was trying to determine where to prioritize its resources, particularly its sales team, as it was trying to scale the business. Our analysis showed that there were markets with certain dynamics that were much more profitable for the company. We also were able to determine which types of merchants were critical to have on both the earning and burn side to drive more traction with the program and the magnitude of the lift it provided. Having high-frequency, necessity merchants led to significantly more traction and created a virtuous ecosystem that made the banks, merchants, and customers all happier.

The end result was a model that predicted revenue, market share, and marketing expenditures to achieve the revenue target the company had promised the state and also the board of directors. The model will be updated now that the property has opened. The resort can use the model both as a scorecard to measure success and as a segmentation strategy in CRM to optimize profitability going forward.

Big data has revolutionized how companies can analyze their business. While having the right technology in place and talented data scientists on staff is essential, being able to interpret those insights with business strategists and turning them into meaningful action is the critical element to driving value.

Doubling Down

- **You've got to have integrated processes in place.** While big data technology has revolutionized what is possible, having the right process between data scientists and business strategists is critical to making effective use of all the information available.

- **Microclusters matter.** They offer sophisticated yet actionable segments that enable marketers to personalize content in a meaningful way to drive more value and loyalty.

- **Crawl, walk, run.** Make progress with the lowest-hanging fruit and show the value of big data—and then evolve.

Interactive CRM

Interactive CRM (ICRM) is the holy grail of marketing, leveraging historical and the most recent information about the customer to customize interactions online, via mobile, and in person in real time. This is an excellent way to maximize inventory utilization from a business perspective, and for customers it should reflect an anticipatory approach to service and their needs. Smartphones and brand-driven apps make this very feasible, though there is still significant work to integrate data from disparate sources to know what to offer and how to redeem it seamlessly for the customer and employee.

We began this journey at Harrah's all the way back in 2003, initially calling it operational CRM. The impetus for this started with an analytic insight that customers who played unlucky—meaning they lost faster than they should normally based on the math of the game (in layman's terms their $100 didn't last as long as they thought it should)—did not return at nearly the same rate as those that had a neutral or winning experience. From a physiological perspective, new customers felt our casino was unlucky to them, and they chose to go back to their preferred casino where they had many winning experiences. Our goal was to intervene during that first trip and provide them with a positive relationship-building interaction to help them feel luckier.

At that point, we created a real-time rules engine to gather information from the casino management system, and we had a series of incentives in our arsenal including coupons to go to the buffet. We did this by triggering an alert to a slot attendant who was told where the customer was playing in the casino, and then the attendant delivered the offer by hand. As this rolled out across the system, we evaluated the improvement in the return rate (customers making a second visit) for those that received the in-trip offer.

Given the initial success, we decided to enhance the ICRM capability to enable us to target existing customers as well. This required us to invest in what at the time was called an active data warehouse so we could get the key subset of customer data available in real time, which we could combine with the gaming data gathered during the trip from the casino management system. We developed a set of interesting scenarios, including going out to celebrate a customer's birthday, or reaching out to those that had given us a bad service score on their last trip, or knowing that customers were approaching their normal playing time. We continued to reach out through human intervention until we developed technology at the game to deliver the message and incentive through an interactive video display at the slot machine. Eventually we moved the incentive to the customer's mobile phone, tested location-based tracking, and expanded offers to include show tickets and the ability to make a restaurant reservation. If we had tickets available to a show that was to go on in a few hours, we could ping customers with an attractive offer, especially if we knew they weren't at one of our properties but were exploring other resorts on the Strip. Or as another example, we could make an offer for the buffet at a nonpeak time, especially if the customers were approaching their normal time limit. Over time we incorporated more of our knowledge of the customers to personalize the incentives even further.

Given we were spending incremental money on labor and the incentives when the guest was already on property, we had to validate if the ICRM channel was driving incremental profitability. To do this we held out 20 percent of the people who qualified as a control group and evaluated three metrics: play during the day of the ICRM offer, satisfaction survey results from that day, and the customer's play over the next 60 days, to determine if there was a longer-lasting impact of a rules-driven positive service interaction. We evaluated this by rule, market, and customer segment to determine which rules were working most effectively and which ones need to be changed or eliminated. We viewed ICRM as a distinct channel just like direct mail, email, and digital advertising, and I put a very talented person, Sandeep Khera, in charge of the channel. He worked collaboratively with the IT, slots, and operations departments to enhance the capabilities and minimize the operational impact and measured the profitability and success of the channel.

Interactive CRM has applications in so many businesses. In sports and entertainment, it could be to upgrade a fan to a better seat that is going unoccupied or to provide real-time stats on a fan's favorite player. In hospitality, it could be an upgrade to a better room. In retail, it could be to recommend the next best product based on what the customers have bought in the past and is on their wish list.

One common saying that comes to mind as it relates to interactive CRM is "Don't let perfection get in the way of progress."

Too often, companies don't execute in this area because there are some missing elements; maybe the companies are missing some data to enter into the rules engine, or they don't have the ability to automate fulfillment of the offer. There is value in executing even with manual work to drive revenue or a relevant customer interaction, and my recommendation would be to follow an iterative model, filling in the missing pieces along the way.

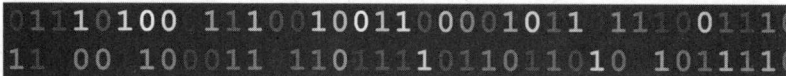

Doubling Down

- **Take a progressive approach.** Executing interactive CRM is very hard, as there are many technical and operational components to consider; adopt a crawl, walk, run approach to gain traction and learn.

- **Treat interactive CRM as a channel.** Have someone own this as a channel, just like you would for more traditional marketing channels, reporting on critical KPIs to show the value being created.

- **Employees can be an effective delivery mechanism.** Enabling employees to build relationships with customers based on "what the machine says" is very powerful.

Putting It All Together

We often dream big at GALE when we start working with great brands, even as we are very focused on delivering value quickly through an iterative approach. However, we do think it is possible to create a highly personalized experience across touchpoints, whether that is in casinos, financial services, healthcare, retail, or even CPG. It starts by putting together a highly skilled and diverse team, including big data experts, strategists, and creatives, that partners with an equally diverse and talented client team. Being able to understand where there are leaks in the client's customer funnel, from awareness to purchase, and being able to quantify it is often a very powerful early rallying cry to define the opportunity and revenue potential.

To prove the value of this more personalized approach, we often start with a pilot that we can execute relatively quickly but is sophisticated enough and built in a way that we can roll it out rapidly to drive value for the client if the agreed-upon metrics are met or exceeded in the pilot. To gather more information from client customers we have found that a quiz that is fun, interactive, and feels natural to customers is a great way to learn more about them. Because it is not a painful survey, customers are willing to tell us more about themselves especially by clicking on product and mood boards in addition to answering a few questions and if we demonstrate that the content is more relevant to them as they progress through their browsing experience. The process starts with a personalized email linking to a landing page that we manage so we can track behavior; various products are shown and inspirational ideas for them to click on and explore are as well. We track this information and use it to develop customer profiles that will drive even more relevant content the next time they come to the website and in emails we send them. In retail examples, this customer-level information is used to create an actionable persona of the customer and helps us ascertain her price point so that we can show her products that are appropriate for her. If her budget is higher, we would show products from higher-end designers. If she is budget conscious, we would show her products that are on the lower end of the available product. We see a significant increase across key metrics, such as open and click-through rates and ultimately more visits and appointments in the store or purchases online, which is the most critical objective with this type of data-driven communication strategy.

The notion of a connected home, or more recently a connected car, has been discussed for several years without gaining significant traction. Part of the reason for that could be that the original ideas came from a technology perspective as opposed to the consumer use case. Take refrigerators as an example; how often would you like to be able to see inside yours when you are at the grocery store to determine if you really need milk? Or when the red filter light on the water dispenser pops on, how valuable would it be to easily send a text to have the new filter sent to you and get an email or text linked to a video for how to replace it? Both are cool, but which is more valuable?

We are starting to see more relevant examples of data connectivity come to light, including at CES (the Consumer Electronics Show) in 2017. Taking a cue from the success of Disney's MagicBand, Carnival Cruises has just launched a device that you can wear as a quarter-sized watch or a necklace that will allow you not only to open your cabin but also to charge food, drinks, retail purchases, and excursions to your account and be kept informed of the day's activities. The cruise staff will know your preferences and itinerary to make informed recommendations that build on what you like or have yet to do. Now this is a strong value proposition for their travelers that leverages data and technology.

It seems that there is a proliferation of connected cars, with Statista reporting that the market for these cars will grow from 12 percent in 2017 to 34 percent in 2021 in what is already a $5 billion business. The question will be how do consumers adopt the technology, and some auto brands are establishing new positions at their dealerships to help educate new buyers, similar to how Apple does with its Genius Bar.

Increasingly we are seeing examples where companies are using data to create more relevant customer interactions. However, it is hard work to get it done, and it requires discipline and focus to achieve it. The benefit is worth the pain, though, as customers will be more loyal to the brands that achieve this success.

01110100 1110 10011 00001011 11 0111
11 00 100011 110111011011010 101111

Doubling Down

- **Match technology with creative chops.** Ascertain pertinent information about customers in a natural way as they explore your site and product, and then use that information to drive relevant personalization.

- **It's all about the customer's point of view.** Developing a connected experience needs to come from a consumer point of view (as opposed to being driven from the technology perspective).

- **Customers are increasingly demanding a more personalized approach.** They want brands that they can interact with and that treat them in a highly personalized way—and they will give their loyalty to brands that can deliver.

CHAPTER
18

Innovation

As demonstrated throughout this book, innovation in the digital and data technology space is happening at a fast pace, and those companies that can innovate, implement, and execute new tools are able to develop deeper relationships with their customers—which in turn will lead to more loyalty and greater profitability. More broadly, as it relates to innovation, there are several epicenters around the world that have the necessary factors, including talent and an investment community eager to fund new ideas. The companies in these epicenters are willing to take calculated risks that enable them to develop new products and services. It is in these epicenters—London, New York, Tokyo, Silicon Valley, Boston, Los Angeles, Singapore, and Paris—where numerous nascent firms have driven radical change across the globe.

Large Companies Struggle with Innovation

Many large companies have challenges driving innovation, often struggling with whether innovation should occur within individual business units or should be driven by a dedicated innovation hub. Creating viable new products and services isn't usually the biggest obstacle to success, but the challenge occurs when an idea has to be transitioned to the proper business unit for full-scale launch and operationalization, according to Innovation Leader, an online resource for people responsible for innovation and R&D. The operational business unit, being involved in the development stage of the innovation is a critical success factor in terms of both creating a product that appeals to the market and predicting the operational implications of scaling it so the business can be prepared to execute. It is essential that the business units have their needs addressed on the front end by the innovation team and that they have skin in the game for the success of the products. It is also important for people from the innovation team to be involved in the transition and rollout to provide continuity and make any adjustments required to scale.

A survey that Innovation Leader did of 164 executives at companies with more than $1 billion in revenue illustrates the challenges of the handoff between an innovation group and a business unit. Around 26 percent of the respondents said the transition from the innovation group to the business unit needs "serious work," and another 16 percent said it was "terrible."

Creating an Innovation Culture

At Caesars, I was part of our Capital Committee, which included the COO, CFO, and CIO. We always made sure that some of our annual capital dollars were allocated to future capabilities and innovation, even though there was a dramatic need for maintenance and physical capital for our casino resorts. Whether it was a cross-functional team or a purposeful innovation team that was put together under the CIO for a period of time, we ensured that the centralized group was well connected with the operators in the development of the ideas, even if we were pushing for something they didn't necessarily know they needed.

Some large companies have gone to the extreme of moving innovation into the business units with some modest central support of innovation process experts. This ensures that the evolutionary idea has business and customer context understanding; the reality is that the personality traits of people who operate versus people who innovate are quite different, as innovators like to explore and ponder new concepts, whereas operators are focused on ensuring efficiency and delivering to meet tangible metrics. Having a blended team is paramount to success no matter which organizational paradigm is used, as creativity needs to be combined with operational reality.

The transition from pilot to rollout is where many companies fail, and both the innovation team and the business unit must have incentives and metrics for success that they strive for and are held accountable for. Understanding how quickly the shift should occur, along with the milestones that determine it, is a skill that large companies need to master to improve their success rate with innovation.

Establishing a culture of driving change and being able to successfully deploy it is a dynamic that many companies struggle with, and there needs to be long-term commitment to make it a reality. Too often, leaders don't recognize or willingly admit there is a need for transformative change until it is too late. Creating an innovation culture enables a company to stay ahead of changes in the competitive landscape and ideally be the driver of that industry change.

New Models for Driving Innovation

Trivergance and its growth engine Ampology have proved there is a new model for big brands to drive innovation. Through uniquely constructed joint ventures and by being an operating partner with expertise in digital and direct marketing, customer acquisition, and the creation of intellectual property, Ampology has created several billion dollars of enterprise value in the past decade with companies such as Verizon and Walmart, leveraging their strong brands but infusing innovation that the companies could not do themselves.

Ampology is the science of accelerated growth, something that many firms need to thrive or even survive. Ampology's unique model is to combine financial, intellectual, and human capital and infuse it into large brand partners. Investing in and creating a mutually beneficial financial structure is combined with well-developed processes to drive innovation and operational expertise to develop a transformative new business that changes the path and story for the partner company. This leads to a significant valuation increase regardless of whether it is a publicly traded or privately held firm.

Previous success stories include Verizon Hum and Diamond Resorts. For Verizon, Ampology developed a connected car solution that provides drivers with a road assistance option and relevant information about their car's performance. For Diamond Resorts, Ampology repositioned the company, led several mergers and acquisitions, and drove more effective marketing to dramatically improve the profitability.

The next example for Ampology is Kazzam by Party City, which will be a platform that connects party throwers with the suppliers of the resources needed to make a party a great success. This will enable the party throwers to enjoy the party experience even more by eliminating the stress and hassle of planning a party, and it will create more joy and happiness in the lives of their friends and family. This will be one of numerous examples of extending the lessons learned of how to use data and digital technology to transform the customer experience and the profitability of businesses at a large scale based on Ampology and Trivergance's past success and financial muscle.

Doubling Down

- **Integrate innovation and operations team.** Regardless of where innovation occurs, from the outset the development of new ideas must be well connected to the business unit that will operate it.

- **Transition is critical.** Most companies fail in the rollout stage. You've got to ensure that the innovation group supports rollout and there is shared accountability.

- **There is a new model.** Large-scale innovation can be successfully outsourced if there is alignment and a strong incentive structure, endorsed by the CEO, working with partners who have demonstrated success building new business units at scale.

CONCLUSION AND EPILOGUE

Stories from My Time in the Gaming Business

I sincerely hope that you have found the experience and examples detailed in the book to be informative and insightful. As you can see, there is a lot that goes into creating a successful marketing organization and great customer experience that permeates throughout all of a company's contact points with its customers. It takes analytic acumen, creativity, and persuasiveness, and above all else, it takes persistence.

It's been quite a journey, and along the way, I have been lucky to work with hundreds of great people who have helped me in myriad ways. I look forward to working with many more in the years to come and helping transform more great companies as they achieve their full potential.

There seems to be a fascination with the inner workings of casinos, and people always ask me for interesting stories about the gaming business. So to conclude, I'd like to share some amusing stories and anecdotes with you about my time in the gaming business; as you can imagine, I was exposed to many fascinating people and situations.

I am sure most of you have seen the *Hangover* movie, which was filmed at Caesars Palace—and which proved to be a great marketing tool for our luxury property. You probably remember

Mike Tyson and his tiger in the movie? Well, we actually did have a high-end customer who was allowed to bring a caged animal to Caesars Palace for his visit. That was just one of many requests that might have raised eyebrows elsewhere, but in our world, they were just par for the course, as our biggest customers were quite demanding and full of unusual requests.

There were so many great experiences that I was fortunate enough to be able to enjoy, including fantastic concerts by artists such as Madonna, Justin Timberlake, Cher, and Elton John. One of the coolest performances I saw was given by Aerosmith in the intimate environment of the bar at the Charles Hotel in Cambridge, Massachusetts, and attending an American Idol finale was exhilarating as well.

We have all had interesting bosses and employees that we have had the opportunity to work with—and I have had my share. I had one direct report who would yell and throw things and would not talk to me for days at a time. I had one boss who, after a long walk together in the woods, had us continue the conversation in a steam room without the benefit of clothing or a towel, leaving nothing to the imagination.

A great story that fortunately I was not privy to firsthand occurred at a company that took the importance of customer service very seriously. Below the VP level, you had to serve on the phones in customer service four hours each month. VPs and above had to listen to calls at least four hours a month. The CEO once took all the people who hadn't served their four hours, admonished them collectively in a large auditorium, and made them put on dunce caps.

When we first started at Harrah's, we wanted to upgrade a quarterly newsletter to a much higher-quality magazine that our customers would value and keep on their coffee tables. Certainly, it was the right choice to switch from our local agency to work with Time's Custom Publishing group, but the decision was made to inform the people at the agency just hours before the grand opening of Harrah's New Orleans. Talk about a downer before what was sure to be an amazing black-tie event!

But fortunately, the positive memorable experiences far out-number the awkward or the bad. Another very neat experience I had was an evening I spent with Johnny Morris from Bass Pro Shops at his Big Cedar Lodge near Branson, Missouri. We were talking to him about developing one of his stores in Atlantic City, right on the water, which would have been a great way to experience and test the boats Bass Pro sells. As we arrived at his resort, we were each given a John Deere tractor that would serve as our mode of transportation to get to the dinner location at the top of the plateau. Every couple of hundred yards there was a painted sign with an interesting message from Johnny. We passed through beautiful caves and incredible vistas on our tractors as we made our way to a breathtaking view at the top where our dinner was taking place. The stories and camaraderie over dinner and by the huge fire pit after were fascinating. Johnny's atten-tion to detail, personal touch, and personality to complement his tough negotiating approach were all apparent, and it is no surprise that the Bass Pro has done so well and is continuing to develop and evolve its experience, as exemplified by the transfor-mation of the Pyramid in Memphis.

Ultimately, you are blessed if you are in an environment where you are doing great things with people you like and respect, as that harmony and symmetry allows you to go well beyond where you could have on your own, further than you ever would have expected. Working with great people doing amazing things is what it's all about. For me it started when I was an intern at

MBNA and then went on to a skunkworks team at American Express that did an incredible project under the radar before we made it more public.

At Harrah's it started with Gary Loveman, Rich Mirman, and me writing our initial ideas on napkins at Memphis Pizza Kitchen. That evolved into being able to work on many projects with so many great people, whether they were on my team, in the field, or partners that we brought in to work with us. Those are the memories that really matter.

And that approach is the energy and vibe we have tried to create with our clients at GALE as we endeavor to transform businesses together by using data and technology to improve the customer experience and marketing effectiveness. We have seen that this can work across a wide range of industries when there is a vision to solve tomorrow's problems today. What started with ideas on a whiteboard has quickly grown into a very unique and robust solution in the services market.

INDEX

About the Author

DAVID NORTON is the Chairman and Chief Marketing Officer of GALE, which helps clients transform their businesses by bringing together the expertise of a top management consultancy with the creativity of an ad agency, backed by strong digital and data analytics capabilities.

Prior to that, Norton spent 12 years at Harrah's/Caesars Entertainment as the Chief Marketing Officer, where he was the architect of the company's loyalty program Total Rewards, its CRM capabilities, and its analytic approach that are well known and respected. He also led brand, advertising, digital, multi-cultural marketing, hotel revenue management, sales, retail, and entertainment. He was recognized as the CMO and Direct Marketer of the Year in 2010 by *CMO Magazine* and *Target Marketing Magazine*, respectively.

Prior to Harrah's he worked at MBNA and American Express, and he is a member of the board of directors of a diverse set of companies including Home Care Assistance, Buzz Points, NVision Lasik Centers, Learners Edge, and Carepoynt. He has a BS in finance from Boston College, an MBA from Loyola in Baltimore, and a masters in technology management from the University of Pennsylvania.